D0571456

Global
GARBAGE

In 1987, this "garbage barge" hauled New York's toxic refuse to Central America and the Caribbean in a futile search for a cheap dump site. Since 1986, toxic wastes of the United States have been dumped in some of the world's poorest countries, including Haiti, Guinea, and Zimbabwe.

Global Garbage

Exporting Trash and Toxic Waste

Kathlyn Gay

An Impact Book
Franklin Watts
New York Chicago London Toronto Sydney

Photographs copyright ©: Capolongo/Greenpeace: frontis; Impact Visuals Inc.: pp. 1 (Kathleen Foster), 7 (Donna DeCesare); UPI/Bettmann Newsphotos: pp. 1 insert, 11, 12, 14; Photo Researchers Inc.: pp. 2 (Maude Dorr), 5 (DeSazo), 6 (J. Allan Cash), 9 (Margot Granitsas), 10 (Peter Gavin); The Bettmann Archive: p. 3; Reuters/Bettmann Newsphotos: pp. 4, 16; Care Photos: p. 8; U.S. Navy Photos: p. 13; NASA: p. 15.

Library of Congress Cataloging in Publication Data

Gay, Kathlyn.
Global garbage : exporting trash and toxic waste / Kathlyn Gay.
p. cm.—(An Impact book)
Includes bibliographical references and index.
Summary: Examines the increasing problems of toxic waste disposal, including such areas as dumping in poor nations, military dumping, and waste disposal in space.
ISBN 0-531-13009-6
1. Hazardous wastes—United States—Management—Juvenile literature. 2. Transboundary pollution—Juvenile literature. [1. Hazardous wastes. 2. Pollution.] I. Title.
TD1030.5.G39 1992
363.72'87'0973—dc20 92-24984
CIP AC

Printed in the United States of America
6 5 4 3 2 1

Contents

Global GARBAGE

Hazardous Exports

"They claim this mother of ours, the Earth, for their own and fence their neighbors away; they deface her with their buildings and their refuse. That nation is like a spring freshet that overruns its banks and destroys all who are in its path."[1]

The great Sioux leader Tatanka Iyotake (Sitting Bull) speaking at a Sioux council in 1877 was reacting to U.S. policies and the federal officials who violated a treaty and ordered the Sioux people to leave their hunting grounds in South Dakota. Today, Sitting Bull's words are a haunting reminder—even a warning—for the world: The industrialized nations are overrunning their boundaries and defacing the Earth with their refuse.

Joni Seager, geographer and editor of a recent publication, *The State of the Earth Atlas*, noted:

> The rich industrial world is stripping the earth of resources and in the course of so doing is generating enormous quantities of effluent and pollution that burden global ecosystems. . . .
>
> Rich countries continue to enhance their wealth by expanding their resource reach beyond their own

borders while frequently exporting their problems . . . choking on a glut of municipal household and industrial garbage, they seek to ship away their waste . . . But this is a small planet . . . there is no "away." There is no safe place to store carcinogenic chemicals, nuclear waste or the toxic by-products of industry.[2]

Consider these examples:

- Highly poisonous mercury from manufacturing plants in the United States and Britain are contaminating a river in South Africa, a river that villagers use for swimming, bathing, washing clothes, and watering cattle.
- Toxic lead from used batteries shipped from Japan and the United States to Taiwan has created serious health problems for Taiwanese workers who break up and burn the throwaway batteries.
- Nuclear wastes, dangerous medical wastes, and hazardous manufacturing chemicals from Germany, Austria, Sweden, and the United States are being dumped in Poland, where people have been struggling for years with health problems linked to poisonous pollutants from their own country's industries.
- Military operations in many parts of the world have produced great quantities of hazardous waste from armaments and equipment that pollute land and waterways.
- Remote areas of the globe such as parts of Antarctica and the Arctic region have become depositor-

ies for toxic trash and oil wastes, threatening fragile ecosystems.

- Even space is littered with debris from space flights and with radioactive materials from orbiting nuclear reactors that could reenter earth's atmosphere and explode.

Toxic trash is not the only kind of hazardous export from the United States and other industrialized nations, however. Dangerous products such as pesticides and medicines that are banned or restricted in the United States are sold to developing nations. And American tobacco companies have developed a vigorous overseas trade in cigarettes, considered health hazards in the United States.

Only recently have governments and citizens worldwide started to take notice of toxic trade and hazardous waste dumping. Some attempts to stop the activities are underway, but illegal and unregulated dumping of hazardous waste and the sale of toxic products continue and may even be increasing. To put it simply: Unwanted materials—the garbage and dangerous products of the industrialized world—have become a global hazard.

MAJOR PRODUCERS AND TRADERS OF TOXIC TRASH

Who produces the most toxic waste? The United States tops the list. The U.S. Environmental Protection Agency (EPA) estimates that Americans generate

270 million tons (240 million tonnes) of hazardous waste annually. But the Center for Investigative Reporting, which conducted a four-year study of international trade in hazardous waste, puts the total at 500 million tons (450 million tonnes).[3]

Most of the dangerous material is disposed of in U.S. facilities, but at least 176,000 tons (158,400 tonnes) are exported annually. Between 85 and 90 percent of these hazardous waste exports go to Canada. At the same time, Canada ships some 55,000 tons (49,500 tonnes) of hazardous waste to the United States each year.[4]

The United States and Canada have signed a bilateral treaty that allows legal trade in waste materials. Under the treaty and current environmental laws in both countries, each nation has to notify the other's environmental agency of the content of waste shipments. If the EPA or Environment Canada decides that a shipment is safe to import, the other country cannot stop the export, even if the exporting nation decides that the shipment contains some dangerous materials.

In both the United States and Canada, some national legislators have encouraged an active trade in hazardous wastes because of the income it provides for businesses on both sides of the border. Several hundred U.S. firms—waste disposal and chemical companies—export hazardous wastes to Canadian companies, and exporters and importers alike have made trade arrangements that are financially beneficial.

U.S. firms, which must abide by strict regulations for disposal of hazardous waste, frequently can ship toxic trash to Canada for treatment at a lower cost than would be possible in the United States. Why? Primarily because Canadian environmental laws are more lenient than U.S. laws, and disposal firms in Canada can operate without installing expensive treatment facilities. For example, Stablex in Ontario, Canada, the nation's largest waste disposal company, which was recently sold to a U.S. firm, operates a landfill for hazardous waste. The landfill would be banned in the United States because it is unlined and toxic materials can easily leach, or seep, through, contaminating the soil and underground water supplies. Tricil in Montreal, Quebec, another large Canadian waste treatment company, burns hazardous waste in an incinerator that would be considered unsafe in the United States, according to environmental groups in both nations.

Some members of the U.S. Congress have proposed laws that would prohibit hazardous waste exports to Canada (or any other country) unless treatment facilities meet standards as strict as those in the United States. But the Canadian government, along with the nation's major importers of hazardous waste, have opposed such U.S. legislation, saying that American standards should not be forced on any other nation. Such standards would infringe on another nation's sovereignty, opponents say.

Another major source of hazardous waste is the European Community (EC), a dozen Western European countries that have agreed to abide by trade laws and other legislation that affects member nations. The EC generates about 35 million metric tonnes (38.6 short tons) of hazardous waste annually. Although there have been efforts to develop standard environmental laws for the EC, great differences exist in what each nation considers hazardous material and how it is treated.

The more prosperous nations have been sending their toxic trash to less affluent countries, which have accepted hazardous waste imports as a way to earn revenue. The United Kingdom and France, however, import most of the hazardous waste from the EC and also accept some shipments from the United States, Canada, and other industrialized nations. British and French waste disposal companies depend on the revenue from toxic trash imports, so they have frequently opposed attempts to decrease international trade in dangerous wastes.

WHAT IS HAZARDOUS WASTE?

In 1976, the U.S. Congress passed the Resource Conservation and Recovery Act (RCRA), which defines hazardous waste as material that endangers human health and the environment (1) because of its chemical or physical characteristics or the amount and concentration of the material and (2) because it is "improperly treated, stored, transported, disposed of, or otherwise managed." Hazardous materials include nuclear wastes, various types of explosives, and infectious materials, along with toxic, or poisonous, chemicals. Obviously not all hazardous materials are toxic, but the terms *toxic* and *hazardous* frequently are used to mean the same thing in regard to wastes.

Many toxic materials are chemical compounds produced in laboratories. At least sixty thousand different chemical compounds have been produced in the United States, but the toxic effects of a vast majority are not really understood. A few have been studied extensively and are regulated. Some have been banned or restricted. According to the Council on Environmental Quality, 14,500 new chemicals have been submitted for government review since 1979, but more than 10 percent have been banned, restricted, or withdrawn from manufacture or use.[5]

Industries that manufacture chemicals, plastics, pesticides, computer parts, prescription drugs, and petroleum products are responsible for releasing a great variety of toxic chemical wastes into the soil, water, or air. Federal law requires industries and businesses to report the kinds and amounts of toxic chemicals released each year. The information is compiled in a Toxic Release Inventory (TRI) that government agencies and environmental groups use to establish protective measures to prevent contamination from toxins.

DANGERS OF SOME TOXIC COMPOUNDS

Dioxin is an extremely toxic chemical compound that forms during manufacturing processes and the burning of various waste products. Some herbicides (weed killers) also contain dioxin.

Actually, dioxin is a group of seventy-five related chemical compounds. The term, however, usually refers to the most toxic form, called TCDD. Most independent scientists consider dioxin the most potent carcinogen (cancer-causing compound) known. Laboratory tests of animals exposed to dioxin show the chemical also is a teratogen; that is, it causes birth defects and other reproductive disorders.

Thousands of studies have been conducted on the health effects of dioxin exposure. The results of one of the most recent was published in 1991 by the National Institute for Occupational Health. The institute's ten-year study of thousands of workers exposed to dioxin in chemical plants found a clear link between dioxin exposure and high rates of cancer among workers.[6]

Yet some chemical manufacturers, officials at the U.S. Centers for Disease Control (CDC), and EPA researchers claim that dioxin is not as toxic as was once believed. In fact, Vernon Houk of CDC has been telling conferences and testifying in court that he considers dioxin only a "weak" carcinogen. Houk says dioxin would cause cancer only in high doses.[7]

There appears to be a concerted effort on the part of some chemical companies and U.S. government officials to develop a media campaign designed to downgrade the risks of dioxin exposure. As one former EPA official explained: "There have been petitions to state agencies, numerous articles written, and litigation—all with the goal of creating the image of a less toxic dioxin. There have been people on both sides of the dioxin debate at EPA since the 1970s, and there have been charges that certain staffers have been linked with [the chemical] industry."[8]

Downplaying the health hazards of dioxin could help companies that are being sued for diseases linked to the chemical. But most toxicologists would agree with Richard Clapp, who directs the JSI Center for Environmental Health Studies in Boston. Clapp says, "Dioxin is still the most potent carcinogen and teratogen ever tested in animals, and the data on humans do not give us any reason to call it [dioxin] 'weak.' "[9]

In July 1991, a St. Louis, Missouri, jury came to the same conclusion after hearing expert medical testimony in a court case involving a worker exposed to dioxin. The victim, Al Overmann, had worked for a small business that sprayed oil laced with dioxin on streets to keep down the dust. He died in 1984 from liver disease and a cancer called soft tissue sarcoma, both associated with dioxin exposure. Defendants in the case, the chemical and petroleum companies that supplied the oil, argued that they were not at fault because they did not actually spray the oil. But the jury found in favor of the plaintiff, Overmann's widow, awarding her $1.5 million. The chemical companies plan to appeal the case.[10]

Chlorine Compounds

Some solvents used in industries are chlorine compounds that cause serious health problems. Chlorine is a natural chemical element that also occurs in combination with other elements, such as sodium chloride (salt) in seawater. In the laboratory, these compounds are broken down to separate out the chlorine and then combine it with other elements to produce a great variety of chemicals. Cleaning fluids like trichloroethylene (TCE) and degreasers like carbon tetrachloride are examples.

PCBs

Other chlorinated compounds produced for industrial purposes include polychlorinated biphenyls (PCBs). PCBs are carcinogens and are linked to birth defects. Once used for insulation in electrical appliances, in hydraulic fluid, and in fluorescent light fixtures, PCBs are now banned in the United States, although many of these chemicals are still around.

Asbestos

Some minerals that are naturally part of the environment, such as asbestos, may be part of hazardous waste materials. Asbestos fibers were once commonly used to make fireproof fabrics, insulation, textured paint, and cement and plaster, but asbestos is now banned in most industrialized nations. The fibers can be inhaled, causing respiratory diseases, including lung cancer.

Mercury

Other dangerous toxins are heavy metals, which also occur naturally in the environment but can be tolerated only in small amounts. Mercury, for example, is extremely toxic. At room temperature, mercury is a colorless and odorless gas that can be inhaled or absorbed through the skin. A person exposed to mercury vapors may exhibit symptoms of poisoning that include nervous tremors (shaking), uncontrollable laughter or crying, and loss of sight, smell, taste, and hearing. Since mercury affects the central nervous system, an extreme case of mercury poisoning can lead to insanity or death.

Another form of mercury is even more dangerous—a mercury compound produced when inorganic mercury (the element without carbon) is released into water. Bacteria in water and sediment alter the element, converting mercury to an organic compound known as dimethyl or methyl mercury. Mercury compounds accumulate in water and become ever more toxic, usually concentrating in the muscles of fish.

The highly toxic effects of the compound became tragically evident during the 1950s, when an epidemic illness spread through a coastal village in Japan. For more than twenty years a chemical plant had been discharging mercury into the sea, poisoning the fish, a staple food for the villagers. Scores of people died or became seriously ill after eating fish contaminated with methyl mercury. Similar cases have occurred in other parts of the world, including the United States. The poisonings have been traced to industrial discharges of mercury into waterways.[11]

Lead

Lead is equally as dangerous as mercury. It was once used in many U.S. products like gasoline and paint but has been banned because of its extreme toxicity. Even low levels of lead can poison. For children, poisoning is defined as 25 micrograms of lead per deciliter of blood, but scientists say this level, once considered safe, will probably be lowered. Studies show that 10 micrograms (one millionth of a gram) or above per deciliter (0.21 pint) are poisonous for children.[12]

Most people are exposed to some lead that is naturally a part of the environment. But lead leaches from car batteries buried in landfills and from old water pipes held together with lead solder. It is released into the air from crumbling lead-based paint and from manufacturing processes in which lead is used. Lead is stored in the body and builds up in bones. Sometimes it is released when bones deteriorate during aging or when bone structure changes such as during pregnancy. Lead poisoning causes anemia, abdominal pains, and fatigue and can lead to brain damage, learning disabilities, and severe neurological problems.[13]

Other chemical elements, such as arsenic, cadmium, chromium, copper, nickel, and zinc, also are found in industrial wastes as well as in soils and waterways near manufacturing plants where these metals are used. Like other metals, they occur naturally but are poisonous when ingested over long periods of time and accumulated in the body.

Problems in Waste Disposal

Within the past decade, many Americans have become aware of the problems associated with disposal of household garbage and trash, usually called solid waste, and hazardous industrial waste. Although household waste usually is not labeled hazardous, it can contain chemical elements and hazardous materials found in household products such as cleaning solvents, drain openers, paint strippers, and pesticides. Toxins collect in leachate, the liquid that seeps from waste while it decomposes. The same is true of ash from waste-burning incinerators, which can contain dangerous chemical compounds that remain or form when trash is burned.

Most solid waste and municipal incinerator ash go to landfills, large pits where waste is buried. But across the United States these sites have been filling up, and only a few new landfills are being built. Federal and state laws require that the landfills be constructed with an underlining of clay or thick layers of vinyl materials or both. They also must be equipped to trap leachate, which could contain toxic materials. Without protective measures, hazardous leachate can drain through soils to aquifers, the underground supplies of water frequently used for drinking. Toxic leachate also can run off into streams and contaminate water supplies.

Requirements for hazardous waste disposal are even more stringent. Usually, hazardous waste sites take industrial wastes, toxic agricultural products, and hazardous building materials such as asbestos. Hazardous waste must be chemically or biologically treated to remove toxins before the waste is dumped; or it must be burned in EPA-regulated incinerators and the leftover ash buried.

DON'T DUMP ON ME!

Some manufacturers and politicians contend that toxic wastes are an inevitable by-product of modern technology and the many conveniences of consumer products and services. Thus, citizens ought to be willing to accept waste disposal sites in their backyards. But public interest groups insist that no one should have to live in an area contaminated by toxic pollutants or with the threat of such contamination. Many citizens have organized to fight toxic waste dumps and incinerators in their communities.

One of the earliest protests against toxic waste was organized in an upstate New York community located near an abandoned waste site called Love Canal. Lois Gibbs, a resident of the community, became alarmed when members of her family and some of her neighbors developed mysterious ailments and several children living near Love Canal were born with physical defects. Gibbs organized a citizens group to demand an investigation, which brought researchers to the abandoned canal. They found the canal once had been used as a dump site for toxic chemical wastes and had been covered over with layers of dirt, a disposal practice thought to be safe decades ago. But the chemicals had contaminated soil and drinking water, creating health hazards.

The discovery at Love Canal led to investigations of other dump sites across the United States. Within a few years more than one thousand waste disposal areas were labeled hazardous. In 1980, Congress passed the Comprehensive Environmental Response, Compensation and Liability Act, which provided a "superfund" for cleaning up toxic waste sites.

Since passage of the Act, now known as Superfund, Congress has allocated $8.5 billion for the cleanup program, but many experts believe it will cost much, much more to decontaminate hazardous waste sites. At the end of 1990, more than twelve hundred sites were on the National Priorities List, which identifies the most seriously contaminated sites. But that number is expected to increase as more waste sites are identified. An estimated 50 percent of all Americans live in counties that contain a hazardous waste site classified as the most dangerous in the United States. And 70 percent of the landfills where toxic trash was dumped in the past are not lined, so poisonous chemicals can leak into the soil, threatening ground water.[1]

For years it has been common practice in the United States to locate garbage dumps and hazardous waste sites in remote rural areas, outside small towns, in poor neighborhoods, or in minority communities. Those responsible for waste disposal know that people in predominately white, middle-class, and wealthy neighborhoods spend time and money organizing protests, but the less affluent are not likely to offer as much resistance. Few have the resources and political contacts to make sure that trash stays out of their backyards.

Several studies within the past decade (the most recent, *Dumping in Dixie* by sociologist Robert D. Bullard, now at the University of California–Riverside) have documented that class and race are major factors in determining where unwanted toxic facilities are placed. People of color and the poor are most often the victims of toxic waste dumping. In fact, some predominately black neighborhoods in Louisiana, Texas, and South Carolina are so contaminated with toxic chemicals that they have become known as "cancer alleys" or "national sacrifice zones."

Numerous grass-roots groups have organized to fight toxic waste dumps and incinerators as well as hazardous emissions from industries. Environmental action in minority communities has been taking place in rural areas, small towns, and cities across the United States. Many grass-roots groups work with the Citizen's Clearinghouse for Hazardous Wastes, which was founded by Lois Gibbs in 1981. The organization helps people help themselves. Field organizers give special attention to low-income, rural, and minority communities, which seldom are represented in mainstream environmental groups.

TRASHING TRIBAL LANDS?

Federal, state, and local legislators have passed many other environmental laws to control the disposal of toxic waste, and public interest groups have continued to protest the placing of waste disposal facilities in their backyards. As a result, waste disposal companies have difficulty finding places to dump garbage and toxic trash. But in recent years, dozens of attempts have been made to place dump sites or build incinerators for hazardous waste on land inhabited by indigenous Americans, which include American Indians and Alaska Native villagers.

More than 300 federally recognized American Indian tribes live on 280 separate reservations in the United States. The lands are held in trust by the federal government. The federal government holds legal title to the lands with an obligation to administer them for the benefit of the people. One of the reservations is located off the mainland on Annette Island, Alaska. Each reservation operates as a sovereign nation with its own tribal government, which, among other responsibilities, has the right to manage the environment.[2]

The federal government also has responsibility to protect human health and the environment on Indian reservations. Federal agencies work with tribal governments on a nation-to-nation (or government-to-government) basis. Indian reservations are not subject to local and state environmental regulations because tribal governments have the power to establish protective laws. But in recent years, amendments to federal environmental laws have made it possible for tribal governments to be treated as state governments in environmental matters. Thus, tribal governments may be eligible for federal grants that can be used to develop codes and regulations. Tribal leaders also work with the EPA to enforce environmental laws.

Alaska Native villagers regulate their 220 villages in a different manner. Under the Alaska Native Claims Settlement Act of 1971, the lands are not in federal trust. They are owned by corporations organized according to state law, with only native Alaskans as shareholders. Although Native villages in Alaska do not have legal authority similar to states, boards of directors of corporations have the right to establish protective measures and regulate natural resources on corporate lands.

In numerous cases, however, state and local governments, and anti-Indian groups that want to abolish U.S. treaties with Indian tribes, have challenged tribal rights. Many state officials are opposed to sharing limited funds for environmental protection with tribal governments. EPA regional offices also have been slow to fully recognize tribal governments. Often federal and state officials ignore Indian leaders, according to directors of the Morning Star Foundation, which works to protect rights of American Indian nations.

Since tribal governments are exempt from state laws and most do not have tough environmental regulations, tribal governments frequently must struggle alone to protect Indian lands from outside polluters. As Morning Star directors explained a few years ago:

> Tribes have been approached by energy and hazardous waste companies promising riches and employment in exchange for allowing hazardous waste sites to be located on their land. The Cortina Indian Reservation bordering California operated an asbestos dump until recently. Without environmental personnel to accurately evaluate the potential cultural and environmental impacts of such ventures, it is possible that more projects such as this may occur.[3]

Indeed, waste disposal companies tried repeatedly in the 1980s to develop hazardous-waste sites on Indian reservations. Examples include attempts to build a toxic-waste incinerator and dump on lands of the Navajo and the Paiute-Kaibab in Arizona, the Kaw in Oklahoma, the Choctaw in Mississippi, the Oglala Sioux in South Dakota, the Mohawk in Canada and New York State, and the numerous villages in Alaska. Although a few Indian leaders have favored the waste disposal operations because of the income they provide, numerous Indian protest groups have organized to successfully stop what has been called a "toxic invasion" of tribal lands.

In one instance, the Navajo community in Dilkon, Arizona, organized a protest under the direction of a community group called Citizens Against Ruining our Environment (CARE) and were able to reject the dumping proposal. CARE and other activist groups held a conference in Dilkon in 1990 to bring together leaders of diverse Indian tribes and build a network to halt the attempts to trash reservations.[4]

THREATS IN THE ARCTIC REGION

Alaskan Natives have to fight not only waste-dumping proposals but also the effects of toxic spills from oil drilling operations and tankers and illegal dumping of oil wastes. At Prudhoe Bay on Alaska's northern coast, for example, drilling waste is routinely dumped on the land and into the sea, killing vegetation, wildlife, and fish.

Oil companies and Alaskan officials, led by Governor Walter J. Hickel with the support of the Bush administration, have been trying to open up the Arctic

National Wildlife Refuge for oil exploration. The area includes a tundra called the Brooks Range in northeast Alaska, which is the home of the Gwich'in, a group of about seven thousand Native people whose ancestors have inhabited the area for ten thousand years. Caribou herds migrate to the tundra, and the Gwich'in depend on the caribou for meat and hides. The tundra wildlife also includes bears, wolves, oxen, foxes, and other animals, as well as many species of birds.

Oil companies also want to drill for oil off the coast of the Chukchi and Beaufort Seas, which has been called "the most ecologically sensitive" area in the Arctic region. Drilling could destroy whales and other sea mammals, as well as the fish and bird populations that Native groups depend on for survival.

Native groups who are part of the Alaska Coastal Policy Council (CPC), a federally mandated organization, have the right to determine what activities take place on their lands. Many CPC members and other activists are concerned about oil spills, which would be unavoidable with drilling, transporting, and processing oil in these frigid regions. Spills on or under ice cannot be cleaned up, and the toxic oil would be a hazard to life in the area for decades.[5]

Dumping on Poor Nations

When manufacturers and waste brokers—traders or agents—cannot find sites for waste disposal in their own countries, they turn to other nations, particularly those not controlled by strict environmental or health regulations. Frequently, such nations are struggling with economic problems. Traders have been able to make arrangements with some less-industrialized countries to import toxic trash because governments and businesses need the money. Traders also arrange highly profitable contracts for their services in handling waste materials from cities, industries, and businesses. Several international organizations have estimated that the toxic waste trade worldwide is a $20-billion-a-year business.[1]

Some countries have banned imports of toxic materials. But at least 10 million tons (9 million tonnes) of hazardous wastes have been unloaded since 1986 in nations that do not have the facilities or money to handle such materials safely, according to Greenpeace, the only international environmental organization that documents the global trade in toxic wastes.

However, Greenpeace believes the total amount of waste exports is much higher because traffic in toxic materials is not monitored regularly and is largely unregulated. Quite often, activities are secret and illegal or are not specifically restricted.[2]

For example, a company attempted to ship New York City garbage to a rural area in Paraguay, South America, offering $6.50 a ton (.9 tonne) for disposal. The company proposed that the trash be used to fertilize the land. However, the head of Alter Vida, an environmental group in Paraguay, said soil in the area was not infertile. Environmental and other citizens groups also suspected that the shipment could contain toxic materials. "When charity is so bountiful, even saints are suspicious," a priest in the area said.[3]

Although Paraguayan law prohibits all waste imports, there is an exception. Some waste can be imported if it can be recycled without endangering the environment or causing human health problems. To date, there has been no decision on whether New York City garbage can be imported as recyclable material.

Labeling materials as recyclable is a common way to dispose of waste that could be harmful. Millions of tons of industrial wastes are shipped to smelters in Asia and Latin America, where wastes are burned to extract various metals. But the recycling process releases heavy metals and other contaminants into the air, water, or land. If there is environmental damage or if people suffer health problems from the toxic imports, little if anything can be done to place blame or to obtain compensation from those responsible.

NO PORT FOR THE *KHIAN SEA*

One of the first series of news stories to shed some light on the shadowy waste trade business began in the *Philadelphia Inquirer* in 1987 and ended more than two years later. Mark Jaffe of the *Inquirer* staff reported on the voyages of the *Khian Sea,* a rusty cargo ship owned by Amalgamated Shipping of the Bahamas. In late 1986, the ship was loaded with nearly 14,000 tons (12,600 tonnes) of ash from Philadelphia's two waste incinerators. The city had a contract with a broker, Joseph Paolino & Sons, to dispose of the ash.

Paolino, who operated a trash transfer station on the Delaware River, made arrangements for the *Khian Sea* to transfer the incinerator ash to a barrier island in the Bahamas. But the Bahamian government blocked the plan, fearing the toxic materials in the ash would harm the environment.

Barred from the Bahamas, the ship began what was to become an epic journey—twenty-seven months of traveling the globe. Greenpeace activists were able to track most of the ship's maneuvering and to alert government officials in various countries about dumping plans. There were attempts to dispose of the ash in the Dominican Republic, Haiti, Honduras, Costa Rica, Guinea-Bissau, the Cape Verde Islands, Chile, Turkey, the Philippines, Indonesia, Bangladesh, Sri Lanka, and Singapore. But no one wanted the cargo. At one port in Haiti, though, workers unloaded several thousand tons of the ash before public protests persuaded the Haitian government to stop the dumping. Haitian officials ordered the ash removed, but the ship left without reloading, sailing out under cover of darkness and leaving its trash behind.

At one time during its travels, the ship returned to the Delaware Bay below Philadelphia. The captain planned to give the ash back to the city or to the trash contractor, Paolino. But before any arrangements could be made, the ship again stole out of port during the night, apparently trying to escape a Coast Guard fine for not reporting a broken depth finder, a navigation instrument.

The ship's name was changed several times during its many slippery maneuvers, and it was sold to another shipping company. By late 1988, Greenpeace spotted the ship, under the name *Pelicano,* off the coast of Singapore. The ship's cargo was gone. Greenpeace believes the ash was dumped in the Indian Ocean, although the ship's captain and the owners deny this allegation.

ILLEGAL DUMPING IN NIGERIA

About the same time that the *Khian Sea* was going through its mysterious changes, the *Karin B,* a freighter with a cargo of highly toxic industrial waste also became a pariah on the sea. Originally, most of the hazardous waste on the ship had come from Italy but had been transported and dumped illegally in Koko, Nigeria. Gianfranco Raffaelli, an Italian businessman, had made arrangements with a Nigerian construction company to be the recipient of the wastes, which were labeled building materials and chemical residues. Raffaelli agreed to pay $100 a month to store barrels of toxic waste on a plot of ground owned by a Nigerian citizen, Sunday Nana.

The deal seemed a bonanza to Nana; it was a way to earn more money than he had ever dreamed possible. But over time the barrels began to leak and to release fumes. Eventually, the Nigerian government sealed off the area and ordered the barrels of waste out of the country. Months passed with no action, so Nigeria recalled its ambassador to Italy and seized an Italian ship in order to force the Italian government to recall its toxic trash. When Nigerian workers finally loaded the hazardous waste onto the *Karin B,* it was evident that the materials were toxic. Some of the workers became nauseated, vomited blood, or were burned by the chemicals. One man was partially paralyzed.

With the potent cargo aboard, the *Karin B* was scheduled to sail for England because the British government had agreed to take the ship's toxic trash. But British citizens demanded that the *Karin B* stay out of British ports, and the ship was turned away. The ship and its cargo also caused public outcries when it tried to dock in French, Dutch, Spanish, and German ports and was refused entry.

Finally, the ship returned to Italy, and workers in protective "space suits" unloaded fourteen thousand barrels of toxic waste, some of it oozing from the drums. Although there has been no report on the final disposal of the hazardous waste, there is speculation that it was burned in an incinerator in Wales, part of the United Kingdom.[4]

In recent years many other ships laden with toxic materials from rich nations have transported their unsavory cargoes to less-affluent countries or to remote areas of the world. For example, a remote area in rural Spain is a disposal site for thousands of tons of hazardous waste shipped there during the 1980s from ten countries, including the United States. The Spanish government encouraged the shipments. Why? Because the government wanted to sell mercury ore from its nationally owned mine. If a manufacturing company bought mercury ore, the Spanish government agreed to take the company's industrial waste that contained mercury residues. A processing plant in Spain would then process the wastes to extract mercury, and the recovered metal would be returned to the manufacturer.

But the recycling operation never got under way. Instead, the waste materials were buried in a landfill near the Spanish mercury mine. The landfill also is near a bird sanctuary and waterways, which could easily become contaminated with mercury draining from the waste. Analysis of soil samples from the area show that concentrations of mercury and other dangerous compounds are much higher than normally occur in soils near the mercury ore mine.[5]

HAULING TRASH SOUTH OF THE BORDER

Large quantities of hazardous materials generated by U.S. companies and cities end up in Mexico. Much of the trash comes from firms in Southern California and Texas. Companies contract with haulers to dispose of hazardous waste, usually arranging for trash to be transported to legal landfills or recycling centers in the United States. But U.S. customs agents and other law enforcement officers have told investigating reporters that some businesses in California ship toxic trash along with other waste materials in railroad cars that travel daily to Mexico.[6]

Some of the toxic trash is trucked into Mexico by haulers who smuggle drums of dangerous debris across the border, sometimes leaving their barrels of poison in abandoned warehouses or dumping them in remote fields, out in a desert, or in ravines. Usually, the haulers offer to dispose of hazardous waste for a much lower fee than would be charged for legal dumping. One California company, for example, paid a waste hauler $12,000 to haul hazardous waste to a U.S. treatment facility, not knowing the material would be dumped in Tijuana, Mexico. Disposing of the material in a legal manner would have cost at least $28,000.

Under the 1976 U.S. Resources Conservation and Recovery Act, a permit is required to dispose of hazardous waste, and smuggling toxic waste is prohibited. But it was not until 1990 that law officials were able to compile enough evidence to bring felony charges against a hauler and his accomplice who were caught smuggling toxic waste into Mexico.

MAQUILADORAS

A large portion of hazardous waste in the border region comes from industries owned by U.S. companies that have located approximately two thousand factories in the area. The factories have been set up under Mexico's economic development plan, which offers incentives such as low import taxes on raw materials and a cheap labor force. Thus, U.S. businesses find it profitable to build assembly plants on the Mexican side of the border. Assembled products are transported back to U.S. plants known as *maquilas*, or "twin plants," where the goods are packaged for sale. But there is little similarity between the Mexican and U.S. plants in the *maquiladora* system, as it is called.

In Mexico, where nearly all of the labor is done, workers receive an average weekly pay of $27 per week. Companies are free to operate without the environmental, safety, and health regulations imposed in the United States. Few if any protective measures are provided for workers who are exposed to radioactive materials, PCBs, methylene chloride, and other toxic chemicals.[7]

Although an agreement between Mexico and the United States requires that toxic wastes from Mexican assembly plants be sent to U.S. treatment facilities, most hazardous materials end up contaminating the environment. Officials of the Mexican environmental agency (called SEDUE) believe that only about a third of the U.S.-owned factories along the border are abiding by environmental laws.

Since the 1980s several environmental and labor groups have been investigating the types of toxic chemicals being released from factories. They also are documenting what happens to hazardous wastes. Abuses include dumping poisonous materials in rivers used for fishing and swimming and as a source of drinking water. Plants also discharge dangerous pollutants into the air or illegally dispose of hazardous waste in open land areas.

The Toxic Campaign Fund, a U.S. environmental organization, recently sent chemist Marco Kaltofen to the border region to collect water and soil samples from twenty-three industrial sites. He found high levels of pollution around most of the industries, including facilities of General Motors and the Ford Motor Company. Kaltofen called the region a "2000-mile-long Love Canal," reporting levels of xylene, a cleaning solvent, in drinking water 6,300 times higher than would be allowed in the United States. Levels of methylene chloride were 215,000 times greater than U.S. water standards permit. Both chemicals are known to cause serious health problems, including cancer.

Workers and their families living in areas surrounding the U.S.-owned factories face many hazards. They raise food animals that drink from water canals contaminated with toxic compounds. Children also play near the canals and frequently around drums of toxic waste. When barrels are emptied, they are used by many families to store drinking water.

Kaltofen reported that "out of the hundreds of waste sites I've visited, I've never seen anything like this, even in the Soviet Union." (Eastern European nations have become known for their extremely high levels of pollution.) Although company representatives said their firms comply with environmental laws, a U.S. EPA official noted that the Mexican government recently closed down a GM plant at the border because environmental conditions were poor.[8]

In early 1991, more than sixty U.S. groups, including environmental, religious, and labor organizations, formed the Coalition for Justice in the Maquiladoras. Its office is at the Interfaith Center for Corporate Responsibility in New York. One of the purposes of the Coalition is to publicize documented cases of environmental contamination and health hazards linked to *maquiladora* activities. The Coalition also encourages stockholders to pressure U.S. companies to comply with health, safety, and environmental standards that are required in the United States.

DUMPING GROUNDS IN THE PACIFIC

International trade in waste affects many other countries struggling with economic problems. A case in point is the Marshall Islands, once part of the U.S. Trust Territory of the Pacific. The nation now has its own internal government, but the United States is responsible for its defense and provides a great deal of financial aid. Attempting to find an independent source of income, the Marshall Islands parliament passed a resolution authorizing two U.S. trash disposal companies—Admiralty Pacific and Micronesian Marine Development (Micromar)—to ship millions of tons of municipal solid waste from the West Coast to the islands. The Marshall Islands government could receive up to $56 million a year as payment for the trash imports.[9]

What would happen to the trash? The U.S. companies proposed that it be used for artificial reefs and to help build up the low-lying islands. The idea was to provide protection from rising sea levels, a possibility often predicted if global warming from the greenhouse effect occurs. (The greenhouse effect refers to the theory that gases accumulating in the atmosphere are warming the earth, which could melt ice caps and raise sea levels, flooding coastal regions and islands in many parts of the world.)

A few legislators in the Marshall Islands objected to the plan. Even if land could be reclaimed, there were no guarantees that the trash used for fill would be free of toxins. One senator said he feared waste disposal companies would hide toxins in the trash in order to profit from the deal.

The senator had good reason for such a suspicion. Investigations of court records in Seattle, Washington, where Admiralty Pacific is located, show that company officials have been convicted of illegal activities. Jim Thompson, head of the company, served a jail sentence for bribery, fraud, and theft. Experts who have studied Thompson's waste disposal plans (as well as those of Micromar) believe they are simply ploys to get rid of trash without meeting environmental regulations. None of the plans contains technical information and data to support the proposal that the waste material could be used safely to build up or reclaim land.[10]

TOXIC SHIPMENTS TO POLAND

Waste traders also have tried to take advantage of Eastern European nations that are having financial problems. Poland is a prime example. The country is trying not only to improve its economy but also to deal with air, water, and soil contamination from its own factories. Several industrial districts and Gdansk Bay in Poland have been called ecological disaster areas, and government officials, along with citizens groups, have been seeking ways to clean up and stop some of the pollution.

When Poland began to develop free trade with the

West in 1989, legislators passed a strict environmental law to ban imports of toxic trash. Included in the ban are shipments of sewage sludge, used batteries, toxic solvents, and residues from steel mills and other industries. However, customs inspectors have had little training in detecting hazardous materials, and toxic waste can easily be disguised as raw materials for reuse or as recyclables, which the law allows.

In a two-year period, from the beginning of 1989 to the end of 1990, firms in Western nations tried to send 22 million metric tonnes (24.25 million short tons) of toxic waste to Poland. Some of the export schemes worked, and more than 46,000 tonnes (50,600 short tons) of hazardous wastes from Germany, Switzerland, Austria, and Sweden entered Poland by illegal or underhanded means.[11]

For example, six hundred barrels of solvents contaminated with dioxin were labeled as products for recycling and were exported to Poland by a German manufacturer. Samples of the solvents, which had been sent earlier for analysis, showed no hazardous materials. But when Polish authorities inspected the residue from the solvent recycling process, they found dioxin and PCB contamination. Polish environmental officials tried to return the contaminated residue to Germany but were unsuccessful.

Officials also tried to incinerate the waste, but Polish farmers in the area where the incinerator was located staged an angry protest. They knew the incinerator could not burn wastes at high temperatures and that the remaining ash would be hazardous. Waste burning also would have spewed pollutants into the air. During their protest, farmers on tractors demolished the incinerator, preventing any further hazardous waste burning at the site.

There have been many other attempts to send toxic waste to Poland, such as schemes to export "harmless" sewage sludge from Denmark and Germany to Polish farms, where the sludge was to be used as fertilizer. Other shipments were supposed to be dumped in a landfill. But the shipments contained toxic heavy metals and other hazardous materials and were refused.[12]

Although plans to trade hazardous waste can be stopped at times, Western companies, including some in the United States, continue to try to find ways to export toxic trash to Poland. Other countries also are pressed to import dangerous debris. "Where there's muck, there's money," as a number of observers have pointed out. But while a few profit, many people around the world wonder why they should be dumped on. Why, they ask, should we suffer the consequences of an environment contaminated with poisons we did not generate?

4 International Agreements on Hazardous Waste

Nations have made some attempts to prevent hazardous waste dumping in remote and poor areas of the world and to stop trade in toxic trash. Usually such efforts involve treaty making, which is a slow and cumbersome process. Delegates from participating nations must hold several conferences to negotiate terms of a treaty and draft a document.

Then the treaty must be ratified, or formally approved, by a designated number of nations, another lengthy procedure. To ratify an international agreement, national government officials must sign the treaty.

In the United States, the Constitution gives the president the power to make treaties. The secretary of state usually negotiates for the president. But an international treaty is also subject to "the advice and consent of the Senate." As spelled out in the U.S. Constitution, two-thirds of Senators present must vote to approve a treaty before it can become effective.

The president then ratifies the treaty by exchanging formal documents with other countries.[1]

The ratification process differs in various nations, and it may take years before all of the required countries have legally approved an international accord. On the other hand, during the past decade, several important environmental treaties were ratified within two or three years. One of those agreements was a global treaty regulating international trade in hazardous waste.

HAZARDOUS WASTE TREATIES

Since 1972, when the United Nations held its first conference on the environment, the UN Environment Program (UNEP) has adopted guidelines for protection of the global environment. These include regulations for shared natural resources, offshore mining and drilling, and marine pollution from land-based sources.

In 1987, the UNEP governing council developed guidelines on hazardous waste, hoping to protect developing nations from toxic materials shipped from the industrialized world. The guidelines provide the basis for an international treaty drafted in 1988. Delegates from more than one hundred nations met in March 1989 in Basel, Switzerland, and signed the protocol. Known as the Basel Convention, it will become effective after ratification by twenty nations.

One provision of the treaty prohibits exporters from shipping waste to another country without the written consent of that country's government. Another provision bans shipments of toxic trash through an intermediary country. If a nation refuses to accept hazardous waste already shipped, the exporting nation must take back the shipment. Other articles define illegal traffic in hazardous waste and require international cooperation "in order to improve and achieve environmentally sound management of hazardous wastes and other wastes."

The treaty does not regulate radioactive wastes, which the agreement said "are subject to other international control systems." In addition, the disposal of wastes from the "normal operations of a ship," also regulated by another international agreement, are excluded from the Basel Convention.[2]

Although representatives of the U.S. government and those of several other industrialized nations praised the treaty, only a handful of countries had ratified the Basel Convention by mid-1992. Most African, Caribbean, and South Pacific countries strongly objected to the treaty, saying it had too many loopholes.

Without an outright ban on hazardous waste trade, corrupt governments could accept toxic trash in exchange for hefty payments, critics say. Greenpeace observers, who attended each negotiation session prior to the final wording of the treaty, said the Basel Convention was really no more than "a simple waste trade notification system."[3]

The treaty allows governments to freely contract with each other to trade in waste and to negotiate agreements outside the treaty as long as those agreements are "not less environmentally sound" than those of the Basel Convention. What is or is not "environmentally sound" could be interpreted in many different ways.[4]

AFRICAN BAN ON TOXIC WASTE TRADE

Because of dissatisfaction with the Basel agreement, member nations of the European Economic Community and less-industrialized nations in Africa, the Caribbean, and the Pacific (known as the ACP nations) negotiated another treaty. Called the Lome Convention, it bans the export of all hazardous waste, including radioactive materials, from the European Community to ACP countries. ACP nations also agreed to prohibit imports of wastes from European countries that are not members of the European Community.[5]

In 1991, the Organization of African Unity (OAU), a political organization that includes all African nations except South Africa and Morocco, went a step further. African leaders who long have opposed what they call "garbage imperialism" said they needed to protect their continent from the industrialized world's hazardous waste. Meeting in Bamako, Mali, OAU delegates adopted the Bamako Convention on the Ban of the Import into Africa and the Control of Transboundary Movement and Management of Hazardous Wastes within Africa.

The Bamako Convention, signed by twelve OAU nations, bans imports of all kinds of toxic waste, including radioactive waste and toxic pesticides. It also bans incineration and dumping of hazardous waste in the ocean.

The treaty sets guidelines for reducing toxic wastes within Africa and calls for the African states to curtail emissions of potentially harmful toxic substances "without waiting for scientific proof regarding such harm." Also, generators of hazardous waste are liable for damages. The agreement is considered one of the most progressive hazardous waste laws in the world.[6]

SOUTH AFRICAN TOXIC IMPORTS

Although South Africa established a policy in 1990 banning hazardous waste imports, the government allows routine trade in wastes from mercury plants. The highly toxic waste imports are labeled "raw material" for reprocessing. Reprocessed mercury is used in the manufacture of rubber and preservatives for paint and wood products.

Thor Chemical, a British firm operating in South Africa, imports mercury wastes for reprocessing. Much of the waste comes from American Cyanamid in the United States and from chemical companies in the United Kingdom.

At Thor, wastes are burned and mercury is recovered from the sludge. But emissions from the incinerator send some of the mercury into the air, and impure mercury from the sludge is buried near the plant. As described previously, exposure to only small amounts of mercury can affect the nervous system, causing tremors, loss of the senses, mental deterioration, and even insanity.

Mercury-contaminated emissions and spills of mercury waste have caused grave dangers for residents of the Umgeni River valley. When it rains, polluted soils wash into the river and travel downstream to the Umgeni River, which runs through KwaZulu villages. The river is the primary source of water for the Zulus and millions of other residents in the province of Natal. People bathe, swim, and wash dishes and clothes in the river.

The South African government's Umgeni Water Board, together with a U.S. investigative reporter and Greenpeace International, conducted investigations that revealed severe mercury contamination of the river. A South African scientist found mercury levels more than one thousand times higher than the World Health Organization's (WHO) safety standard of one microgram of mercury per liter of drinking water. Sediment samples show that mercury levels were 8,810 times higher than standards set by the U.S. EPA for mercury wastes. In addition, tests clearly linked the mercury to waste discharges from Thor Chemical.[7]

ENFORCING BANS ON WASTE TRADE

The practice of trading in hazardous materials for reuse has become increasingly common around the world as cases in Europe and the South Pacific have demonstrated. Waste traders also have tried repeatedly to convince Caribbean countries to accept toxic trash for reuse. One plan was to build incinerators to burn waste and produce electricity. The leftover ash would be used to build roads. But traders did not reveal that emissions from an incinerator could pollute the air, and the ash could contaminate the soil with heavy metals and dioxin.

Caribbean nations, along with eight countries in the South Pacific that signed the Lome Convention, have rejected most such proposals. However, several dozen South Pacific and Asian countries have no restrictions against hazardous waste imports of any kind. Thus, attempts are underway to expand the Lome Convention and create a regional ban on waste imports. In fact, Latin American and Caribbean officials met in the latter part of 1990 to discuss ways to protect the region from all types of toxic waste.

Enforcing international treaties may be as difficult as (or even more difficult than) adopting such agreements. Are there ways to make sure that nations comply with international standards?

Some UN delegates have called for an international authority to enforce global environmental agreements. But others believe that some regulations can be set by international technical organizations. Even though such regulations are not mandatory, nations will abide by them. Such is the case with WHO guidelines for health practices, which have been used as a basis for many nations' public health programs. In other instances, regional environmental agreements have included regulations for protection of the seas. Participating nations have not formally agreed to the regulations but have accepted them as standards for their own countries.[8]

National governments also help assure compliance with treaties. In the case of trade in hazardous waste, some countries not only pass laws to ban such trade but also to control hazardous materials within a nation. Canada, for example, has passed legislation to destroy all PCBs by 1996 and to reduce all kinds of wastes by 50 percent before the new century begins. In the United States, legislators recently have introduced bills that would limit hazardous waste exports to countries that have environmental standards comparable to U.S. standards.

Nongovernmental organizations have played a major role in restricting trade in hazardous waste. Environmental groups such as the World Resources Institute, the World Wildlife Fund, the Sierra Club, the Natural Resources Defense Council, and Greenpeace have publicized many of the hazards to the global environment and have pressured legislators to pass protective laws. Greenpeace's Waste Trade Project has documented more than one thousand attempts among industrialized nations to export waste. Publicizing these practices has alerted countries to the dangers and helped stop the import of some shipments.

5 Exporting Toxic Products

Some government officials in less-industrialized countries and environmentalists and health workers worldwide have called for restrictions on another type of toxic trade. It is trade in products that are prohibited or restricted in the nations in which they are produced.

What prompts this kind of toxic trade? When companies cannot sell their goods to consumers in their own countries, they may lose money. But billions of dollars can be earned selling hazardous products to overseas consumers, who may be unaware of the dangers posed by the goods they buy and use.

ASBESTOS

Canada is a major producer and exporter of a hazardous product: asbestos, a natural mineral fiber. Asbestos has been used in insulation and fireproofing materials for many years, but when these construction materials age, they sometimes decay and crumble, releasing asbestos fibers and dust. If asbestos particles are inhaled, they can cause lung and intestinal cancer, and people who work in asbestos mines are at high risk of dying from asbestos exposure.

The Canadian government insists that the type of asbestos mined in Canada—called chrysotile or white asbestos—can be used safely if precautions are taken. Chrysotile asbestos, Canadians claim, is not as harmful as other types of asbestos used in building materials. But health experts at the U.S. National Academy of Sciences say that any asbestos exposure is dangerous. U.S. laws restrict imports of Canadian asbestos, with a near total ban to take effect in 1997.

Canada promotes the development of manufacturing firms that make products with asbestos, and it exports nearly half of its asbestos to less-developed countries. Canadian promotional efforts have helped boost asbestos exports to third world nations. For example, exports to South Korea rose steadily from 5,000 tons (4,500 tonnes) in 1980 to 44,000 tons (39,600 tonnes) in 1988. During that same period, exports to Pakistan increased from 300 tons (270 tonnes) to 6,000 tons (5,400 tonnes).[1]

Although Canadian officials claim they train workers in third world countries to use asbestos safely, poorer countries do not have the funds to regulate asbestos use or to provide safety equipment. According to a report in *The Wall Street Journal*, asbestos dust from one factory in a South Korean village covered the walls of nearby homes. "The plant's 300 workers, unaware of the risks, all had asbestos fibers in their phlegm. When the town complained, the factory's operator erected a higher wall—a futile barrier against clouds of dust."[2]

LEADED GASOLINE

For more than twenty years, countless newspaper and magazine articles, as well as scholarly studies, have outlined the dangers of lead. The U.S. EPA has warned that lead particles in vehicle exhaust emissions are the greatest cause of lead accumulation in humans. Since the 1970s, U.S. automakers have been manufacturing cars that are designed to operate on unleaded gasoline, and in 1985, the EPA banned most lead additives in gasoline, allowing only .10 gram (.0035 oz.) per gallon. As a result, the use of leaded gas dropped significantly in the United States, and U.S. oil companies began exporting leaded gasoline to third world nations, earning $1 billion in sales annually.[3]

According to a report by Christopher Scanlan of the Knight-Ridder News Service, the exporting companies include Octel, a multinational corporation with headquarters in London, England. Octel is owned by two U.S. firms, Great Lakes Chemical and Chevron, and by Royal Dutch/Shell. Other exporters are Ethyl Corporation, which owns a refinery in Ontario, Canada, where lead is added to gasoline, and Du Pont, a U.S. chemical manufacturer that owns a plant in Mexico. Du Pont produces lead additives in cooperation with the Mexican oil industry.

Oil refiners claim that their product is needed because many older cars that operate on leaded gas are still being used in developing countries. An Octel spokesman even argued that the health hazards of leaded gasoline have not been proved.

However, two researchers at the U.S. government's Oak Ridge National Laboratories in Tennessee recently reported that in the United States alone between 3 million and 4 million children are affected by lead poisoning. Each year, another four hundred thousand fetuses are at risk because of exposure to lead before they are born. With increasing exports of leaded gasoline, countless children in Asian, African, and Latin American countries certainly will be poisoned as well.[4]

CIGARETTES

Warnings about the health hazards of smoking are familiar. Many health experts consider cigarettes among the most lethal commodities ever produced. The World Health Organization has calculated that if global smoking patterns persist at the present rate, about one-tenth of the world population now living will die from tobacco-related diseases. Until about 2020, most of the deaths from smoking are expected to occur in industrialized countries. But by 2050, deaths due to tobacco could top 10 million each year, and 70 percent of those who die will be in less-developed countries.[5]

Since the 1980s, there has been a steady decline in the number of Americans aged eighteen and over who smoke. But the sales of U.S. tobacco products are increasing overseas, particularly among young people. Some health officials and consumer advocates are convinced that the increase in cigarette exports is due to U.S. trade practices and aggressive advertising designed to encourage tobacco sales abroad.

The United States has pressured Asian countries such as Taiwan, China, and Japan to accept tobacco products in order to counteract trade surpluses. In other words, Asians sell more of their goods to Americans than the other way around, and the United States wants to create a better balance of trade.

In 1987 negotiations with Taiwan, U.S. trade officials argued that American tobacco products could not compete with Taiwanese tobacco products unless U.S. companies could advertise. Although Taiwanese law prohibits cigarette advertising, U.S. trade officials threatened to curb imports of Taiwanese products into the United States, which helped U.S. companies win approval to advertise their tobacco products on a limited basis in Taiwan. But Taiwanese government officials and a consumer group called the Asian-Pacific Association for the Control of Tobacco say the advertising has been excessive.

In one promotional campaign, young women in mini-skirts stood on street corners near high schools and colleges, handing out free samples of American cigarettes. In another advertising effort, a U.S. tobacco company gave away free disco tickets in exchange for empty cigarette packages. The Taiwanese believe such aggressive advertising and promotion have been responsible for a significant increase in the number of teenage smokers in Taiwan, and for several years the Asian-Pacific Association has been campaigning to curb imports of U.S. cigarettes.[6]

Louis W. Sullivan, U.S. secretary of health and human services, has condemned tobacco companies that profit from the sale of cigarettes while endangering Americans' health. But Sullivan has not criticized the U.S. policy of promoting the export of cigarettes. He and other Bush administration officials have said repeatedly that cigarette exports are trade matters.

And according to news reports, Vice President Dan Quayle, in a speech before a Republican group in mid-1990, said, "[U.S.] tobacco exports should be expanded aggressively because Americans are smoking less."[7]

When asked about the morality of exporting a lethal product, some federal government officials conceded that the United States may have an obligation to provide information about health hazards of some products. But those who support federal trade policies say it is not a U.S. responsibility to decide whether nations should import dangerous products. Besides, they argue, if countries do not buy tobacco products from the United States, they will buy them from other countries.

EXPORTS OF OTHER DANGEROUS PRODUCTS

Government officials and manufacturers have used the same type of argument to justify exports of other dangerous products that cannot be sold in the United States. These have included sleepwear for infants treated with a fireproof material that can cause cancer and contraceptive devices that cause a variety of health problems.

Medications that have been banned in the United States are exported also. For example, the painkiller dipyrone, which can cause a fatal blood disorder and was banned in 1977, is still being sold in Mexico.

Another health remedy, Imodium, made by a subsidiary of Johnson & Johnson, has been used in developing countries to treat infant diarrhea. But the

World Health Organization has warned since 1980 that Imodium can damage a child's intestines. Seven babies in Pakistan died after they were treated with the medication, and doctors asked the manufacturer to remove Imodium from stores. But the company took no action until after a British television program showed pictures of the dying infants.

The United States is not the only industrialized nation that exports banned medicines, and multinational companies often have subsidiary firms in countries around the world. So it is impossible to know how many banned medicinal products are exported to or manufactured and sold in countries where people are not aware of the dangers of the drugs.

THE "CIRCLE OF POISON"

Pesticides, which are designed to poison or kill unwanted insects, rodents, bacteria, and other organisms, are perhaps the most widely publicized toxic exports. An estimated forty-five thousand chemical pesticide products, which include insecticides (to kill insects) and herbicides (to kill weeds), are produced in the United States. Federal and state laws prohibit the sale and use of pesticides that have been analyzed and found hazardous. But unfortunately, the majority of pesticides being sold today have never been registered or tested for adverse health effects. Some cause environmental damage, such as massive deaths or malformations of fish and birds, or are linked to human cancers, reproductive disorders, damages to the nervous system, and other serious health problems.[8]

Yet some banned pesticides, along with unregistered pesticides, can be sold to other nations. The pesticide DDT is a notorious example. The United States and Britain ban the product for domestic use, but over the past decade exports of DDT to less-developed countries have risen dramatically.[9]

DDT and other highly toxic pesticides contaminate the environment and jeopardize the health of many agricultural workers. In poor countries, workers are not adequately protected when they use any hazardous pesticide. They cannot afford to buy masks and gloves, usually the minimum precaution when applying toxic chemicals. Few workers can read product labels and have not been told about the dangers posed when using pesticides. Many labels do not even warn that the chemicals could cause cancer, birth defects, nerve damage, or other serious ailments.

In developing countries, there are few if any regulations on how pesticides should be applied. There are no funds to provide education on handling, storage, and disposal of dangerous products. Frequently, workers use empty pesticide containers for household purposes such as storing drinking water.

The World Health Organization has estimated that each year 25 million agricultural workers in developing nations are poisoned by pesticides. Cases of pesticide poisoning average sixteen thousand per year in a nation like Sri Lanka and about fifteen thousand annually in El Salvador.[10]

The pesticides also endanger Americans. Workers in chemical plants that produce hazardous pesticides may suffer health problems because of exposure to toxins. And residues of pesticides used in farming overseas may remain on food products that the United States imports. Thus, pesticide exports create "a circle of poison," a term popularized when a book with that title, written by David Weir and Mark Schapiro, was published in 1981.

In January of that same year, after intense pressure from various activist groups, President Jimmy Carter issued an executive order forbidding the export of toxic pesticides and other hazardous products. But his order was revoked by President Ronald Reagan when he took office. Reagan advocated deregulation of business during his eight years in the presidency. According to administration policy, American companies would be at a disadvantage if pesticide exports were prohibited, and U.S. companies would not be able to compete with foreign companies in the world market.

Similar policies have continued under the presidency of George Bush. Critics say these policies are designed to favor business interests and the free trade of certain hazardous products. Although exporters must provide the EPA and importing countries with information about the kinds of banned products being exported, the EPA does not have the authority to prohibit exports. In fact, federal policies in regard to hazardous products set a double standard. Laws are designed to protect Americans from exposure to toxins and other hazards, but no laws prohibit the export of toxic products to other countries.

PESTICIDE EXPORTS

The export of toxic pesticides has been proceeding rapidly over the past few years, according to the Foundation for Advancement in Science and Education (FASE). Studying thousands of pages of U.S. Customs documents, FASE found that in just a few months, from March to May 1990, American pesticide manufacturers exported "extremely toxic and U.S.-banned pesticides to developing countries at a rate of at least 2.5 tons (2.25 tonnes) each hour."[11] Shipments were sent to dozens of countries.

Chlordane was one of the products exported. Considered one of the most highly toxic pesticides ever produced, chlordane tends to accumulate in human fat tissue. The National Academy of Sciences says there is no "safe" dosage of the product. But chlordane has not been banned in the United States. Instead, the EPA has restricted its use.

In 1987, Velsicol Chemical Corporation, the only manufacturer of the product, was allowed to sign an agreement saying the company would stop selling the pesticide in the United States. That did not slow production of the pesticide or sales to other countries, however. The FASE investigation showed that "in the years since withdrawing chlordane from the U.S. market Velsicol has dramatically increased shipments of technical grade chlordane [the chemical in its pure form] to foreign ports, from an average of approximately 440 to more than 5,000 pounds (198–2,250 kg) per day."[12]

Aldicarb is another extremely dangerous pesticide that is being exported. The pesticide is banned for use on some food crops but is registered for use on a variety of fruits and vegetables grown in the United States and in other countries. However, "aldicarb has caused numerous worker poisonings," according to the Pesticide Action Network (PAN), an international activist group with a North American regional office in San Francisco. PAN has called for a worldwide ban on aldicarb.

When aldicarb was used illegally on a watermelon crop in California in 1985, an estimated one thousand people in several western states and Canada were poisoned after eating the contaminated fruit. Between 1980 and 1986 in California, aldicarb ranked seventh as a cause of pesticide poisonings that required hospitalization. Aldicarb can cause a variety of disorders, including diarrhea, seizures, and respiratory ailments; poisoning may even lead to death. "In addition to its acute health hazards, aldicarb also poses serious environmental hazards. It is highly toxic to mammals, birds, and aquatic organisms and has been found to contaminate groundwater in at least 22 states," PAN says.

In 1991, aldicarb residues were found on bananas sold in Latin American markets. The residue levels were as high as those on the poisoned watermelons in the United States. According to PAN, the major banana-producing companies spent an estimated $100 million to recall aldicarb-treated bananas, and the U.S. firm Rhone-Poulenc, the lone manufacturer of the pesticide, said that it would withdraw the sale and use of aldicarb on bananas. But the company continues to sell the pesticide for use on other crops.[13]

Parathion is one more highly toxic pesticide export that PAN and other activist groups would like to see banned worldwide. Since the 1970s, parathion reportedly has caused numerous deaths among agricultural workers, and in early 1991, the U.S. EPA announced plans to ban the product. Cheminova, the Danish manufacturer of parathion, is fighting the ban because the company exports $10 million worth of the pesticide to the United States each year. Yet Cheminova withdrew parathion from the Danish market in 1990.

In mid-1991, a CNN-TV "Special Assignment" focused on former EPA officials who now work as consultants for Cheminova. The company says parathion is safe to use if applied according to label directions and claims there have been no injuries linked with parathion use in the United States over the past two decades. However, the EPA issued a report in 1986 that warned of parathion poisonings "among all categories of workers who come into direct contact with the insecticide" and added that "poisonings occur under the most stringent protective conditions." The agency concluded: "Little or no margin of safety exists for parathion use."[14]

Some free-trade advocates dismiss the hazards of pesticide exposure, saying the health risks are minimal compared to the risks of possible food shortages. Pesticides are essential, it is argued, to increase food supplies in developing nations.

However, experiments in Asian, African, and Latin American countries, as well as in the United States, have shown that crop yields do not have to decrease when chemical pesticides are reduced. Growers who use practices known as integrated pest management (IPM) are able to maintain high yields. In brief, IPM techniques make use of natural predators and parasites; that is, beneficial insects and other organisms are encouraged to multiply and feed on pests that destroy crops. Growers also rotate crops—change the kind of crop grown in a field each year or every other year—and use a variety of other techniques to maintain crops without chemical pesticides.

This boy's family and neighbors had to abandon their homes, because they bordered Love Canal. The canal had once been used as a dump site for toxic chemical wastes. It then had been filled in with layers of dirt, and homes were built on it. Twenty years later, in the 1970s, the buried chemicals began to surface, as in these backyards, and to contaminate the soil and water. Of the eighty chemicals buried, eleven were carcinogens.

Hazardous dumps are often placed near poor communities. Predominantly white, middle-class, and wealthy neighborhoods spend time and money to protest the location of toxic sites near them, but people in poor neighborhoods or minority communities are not able to offer as much resistance.

United States trade practices and aggressive advertising are responsible for the increasing sales of American tobacco products overseas. Health officials calculate that about one-tenth of the world's population now living will die from tobacco-related diseases.

Companies exporting waste have tried to take advantage of Eastern European nations that are having financial problems. This dump in Czechoslovakia is considered to be one of the most perilous toxic dumps in Europe.

Industrial chemical runoff was responsible for these dead fish in the Seine River in Paris.

In Sri Lanka, each year there is an average of 16,000 cases of pesticide poisoning among workers such as these women transplanting rice seedlings.

On this plantation in Costa Rica, the bananas are covered with plastic bags containing insecticides and herbicides, and crop dusters spray the fields (where the workers live) regularly. The poisonous pesticide aldincarb, made in the United States, was found on bananas sold in Latin America.

Twenty-five million workers in developing nations, such as these women planting in Chad, are often poisoned by pesticides that are banned in the United States but can be exported to less developed countries.

Although it is an idyllic scene to the eye, tanker accidents, refinery wastes, and toxic waste dumping have polluted much of the Mediterranean Sea.

The ocean appears beautiful, but since the open seas are not owned by anyone, nations use these bodies of water as global garbage cans or open sewers.

Medical debris washing up on beaches prompted the U.S. Congress to ban ocean dumping of any wastes as of 1991. This health department inspector holds a discarded syringe that was washed up on the beach.

In 1989 the oil tanker *Exxon Valdez* spilled 11 million gallons (42 million liters) of oil in Alaska's Prince William Sound. These dead sea otters are covered in oil from the ship's holds.

The Arctic appears to be pristine snow and ice, but under the ice, fragile ecosystems are threatened by polluting oil spills and drilling explorations. Oil on or under the ice cannot be cleaned up and remains a hazard for decades.

Some of the most polluted sites in the United States are military bases and nuclear weapons plants. Rocky Flats nuclear weapons plant near the Colorado Rockies is under investigation for its handling of hazardous materials.

More than 6.5 million pounds of debris from manufactured items streak around the planet, endangering spacecraft and astronauts in flight. Scientists fear that the $1.5 billion Hubble Space Telescope launched in 1990 could be severely damaged by space debris during its seventeen-year life-span.

At a garbage dump near Beirut's International Airport, children pick their way through the garbage with claw-axes, seeking items to sell.

Although chemicals may be used in an IPM strategy, they are usually applied only as a last resort and not, as is now recommended, for conventional farming methods. In conventional applications, growers use pesticides on a regular schedule during a season regardless of whether pests are endangering crops. As a result, beneficial insects are destroyed along with harmful ones, and new pests that resist pesticides come along to take over.[15]

Although pesticides are used on crops grown for local consumption in developing countries, most of the pesticides are applied to export crops—coffee, sugarcane, bananas, and cotton, for example. These crops go to affluent nations such as the United States and Japan.

According to the FASE report, a "growing coalition of environmentalists, academics, and legislators" are determined to bring about U.S. policy changes in regard to the increasing export and use of hazardous pesticides. A panel of scientists and researchers from a variety of disciplines is compiling and distributing accurate information about pesticide exports and advising government leaders about ways to reduce pesticide poisoning. "Both industry and government need to adopt policies which clearly demonstrate that our public health concerns extend beyond our own borders," the FASE report concluded.[16]

BREAKING THE CIRCLE OF POISON?

Senator Patrick Leahy of Vermont, along with other federal lawmakers, introduced a bill in 1990 that would help break the circle of poison. The bill was defeated but was reintroduced in 1991 as the Circle of Poison Prevention Act. During congressional hearings on the bill, Leahy charged that U.S. chemical companies "in the blind pursuit of corporate profits" have ignored their own scientific studies that show the acute, or severe, toxicity of some pesticides. Companies have "dumped their poisons overseas and devastated the lives of thousands of unsuspecting and innocent people," the senator said.

Leahy called attention to DBCP (1, 2-dibromo-3-chloro propane), a pesticide banned for use in the United States because it can cause sterility. Even though the pesticide is no longer manufactured, "the tale of DBCP is an appalling one," Leahy said.[17]

DBCP was widely used in banana fields in Costa Rica and has been blamed for causing sterility among Costa Rican workers, several of whom are suing Dow Chemical Company and Shell Oil Company, manufacturers of DBCP. One worker said that the only safety advice he received was to carry water to wash away the chemical if it splashed on him.

Catharina Wesseling of the National University in Costa Rica has been coordinating research on pesticide abuses in Central American countries. Testifying before the U.S. congressional committee, Wesseling said that pesticides are being touted as a way to help Central America become a major exporter of agricultural crops. This in turn could help the region get out of its tremendous debt. But farm workers are bearing a great deal of the cost. University researchers have documented many human poisonings due to pesticide exposure. Wesseling said the poisonings caused serious illness and death among agricultural workers and their families. The pesticides have contaminated waterways and have sickened and even killed animals. "We have found pesticide use in all the Central American countries to be intensive, extensive and thoroughly out of control," she said.[18]

6 Ocean Dumping

While governments and citizens groups worldwide are just beginning to focus attention on trade in toxic waste and hazardous products, another global dumping problem has been under investigation for several decades: disposal of hazardous materials at sea. Since the open seas and oceans are not owned by anyone, nations use these water bodies as global garbage cans or open sewers. Industrial countries worldwide contribute to the problem.

Vast amounts of contaminating sewage, industrial wastes, and dredgings (soil sediments dug from waterways) have been dumped regularly from barges and ships into the oceans. Plastic throwaways, such as garbage bags and six-pack holders, and huge fishing nets have entangled and destroyed dolphins, sea lions, turtles, waterfowl, and other aquatic animals. Oil spills and petroleum wastes have endangered sea life and coastal areas in many parts of the world. In addition, hazardous pollutants from land-based sources endanger or destroy offshore areas near most industrial countries.

BANS ON OCEAN DUMPING

In 1972, representatives of ninety nations met in London to negotiate a treaty regulating ocean dumping. Known as the London Dumping Convention, the treaty requires each participating country (which includes the United States) to set up a system for controlling any materials that may be designated for disposal in the ocean.

The London Convention regulates pollution from ships, oil rigs, and other marine sources. It prohibits the disposal of certain toxic substances such as mercury and cadmium compounds in the oceans. Dumping high-level radioactive wastes is also forbidden.

High-level radioactive waste comes from nuclear weapons and power plants. The problem of nuclear waste disposal has been festering since the United States began to build atomic bombs in the 1940s. An atomic bomb explodes because unstable uranium atoms split. As they split they release neutrons, tiny atomic particles, which in turn hit other uranium atoms, fissioning them in a continual chain reaction that creates more and more heat and eventually causes an explosion. Nuclear fission also supplies energy, or electrical power.

Radioactivity begins to take place as soon as an atom splits, releasing energy (radiation) in the form of particles or rays. If high amounts of energy are released, the radioactivity can damage living tissue and cause cancer and birth defects. Intense radiation may cause death.

Whenever nuclear weapons and energy are produced, the byproducts are radioactive waste. Some of the waste may remain radioactive for thousands or even millions of years. Such materials are stored in tanks or protective pools of water or are "glassified," mixed with clay or sand and melted to form a glasslike substance when it hardens inside steel cannisters. But these methods of disposal are only temporary, and nations that produce nuclear waste must find permanent sites for radioactive waste materials. For a time, the vast oceans seemed like safe depositories. But radioactive materials can cause serious problems for marine life, such as deformities and cancer.

Although the London Convention forbids dumping of high-level radioactive waste in the ocean, a major and continuing controversy has been the question of whether low-level radioactive wastes should be dumped at sea. Low- or medium-level wastes include such things as discarded gloves and clothing used by nuclear plant workers, radioactive materials from hospitals and laboratories, and some waste from power plants.

A number of European nations regularly dumped low-level nuclear wastes in the North Atlantic Ocean until 1983. That year the London Convention passed a resolution calling for member nations to voluntarily suspend such dumping. Several countries tried to ignore or circumvent the resolution, but citizen protests brought a stop to the nuclear waste dumping.

Over the past decade, there have been proposals to experiment with disposal of nuclear waste and other toxic trash *under* the seabed, gaining access via tunnels from land. Such a method is not controlled by international law; the London Convention regulates only waste dumping from ships or other marine sources. Some northern European nations want the practice covered under the Paris Commission, an international regulatory council that controls pollution of the North Atlantic, North Sea, Arctic Ocean, Barents Sea, and Greenland Sea from sources on land.

At a meeting of the Paris Commission in June 1991, however, the participating nations did not adopt regulations. But the conferees did agree that if radioactive waste from land sources is buried under the seabed, it might be a source of marine pollution. Representatives also were in accord that the Paris Convention was an appropriate body to regulate such waste disposal.[1]

DEBATES OVER BURNING TOXIC WASTES AT SEA

Nations have not been able to reach agreement on the practice of burning hazardous wastes at sea. Several European nations burn wastes in incinerators on ships, dumping the ash into ocean waters. Some experts insist that ocean incineration is safe and that it is the most cost-effective way to dispose of millions of tons of hazardous wastes that are generated each year in industrial nations. Proponents claim that when modern incineration equipment is used and burning is handled correctly, all but about .0001 of the material is destroyed. But that can result in a ton of waste left over after burning 10,000 tons (9,000 tonnes).

Critics of ocean incineration point out that even small amounts of unburned hazardous wastes can accumulate in marine organisms. Another danger of burning hazardous wastes at sea is the possibility that an incineration ship might accidentally leak, which could be a major catastrophe. The EPA once warned that a ship's cargo of PCBs would be capable of damaging or destroying all life in the Gulf of Mexico.

Nevertheless, a U.S. firm, Waste Management, Inc., the largest waste-handling company in the world, was allowed to use a location in the Gulf of Mexico for experimental burns of liquid hazardous waste. But citizens living along the Gulf organized massive protests against the practice, and a federal court decision extended the 1988 Ocean Dumping Ban Act to cover incineration at sea. In early 1991, the EPA ordered the Gulf burn site closed.[2]

U.S. LAWS AGAINST OCEAN DUMPING

More than a dozen U.S. laws directly or indirectly govern ocean dumping. Some laws regulate offshore drilling for oil, which may be responsible for spills. Others protect marine mammals and other aquatic life from pollution.

The U.S. Water Pollution Control Act of 1972, which was later amended by the Clean Water Act of 1977, provided grants to cities to improve their waste-treatment facilities and included regulations for disposal of industrial wastes into the nation's rivers, lakes, and sea waters. The law also regulates the disposal of soil sediments dredged from bays, harbors, and other water bodies to deepen them. Frequently, these dredgings contain heavy metals and other toxic substances, and the EPA determines where the sediment can be dumped: in a deep-sea basin, a land area, or other site.

Congress passed the Marine Protection, Research,

and Sanctuaries Act of 1972, known as the Ocean Dumping Act, which was amended five years later to ban the dumping of sewage sludge into the ocean by 1981. But New York City challenged the law, arguing that there was no available land site for sewage sludge from the metropolitan area. The city was able to continue the practice of dumping 6 million tons of sludge into the ocean each year in an area 115 miles (185 km) offshore.

Although the EPA reported no evidence of damage to marine life in the area, the agency found toxic metals and high levels of harmful bacteria in the waters at a former dumping site 10 miles (16 km) offshore. Adverse effects on marine life, as well as medical debris and other trash washing up on beaches, prompted the U.S. Congress to pass the Ocean Dumping Ban Act of 1988. The Act became effective at the end of 1991 and prohibits ocean dumping of any wastes from U.S. sources.

In addition to the ban on ocean dumping, 1990 amendments to the Coastal Zone Management Act require coastal states to develop programs to control pollutants that enter the ocean from diverse sources (often called nonpoint pollution). These sources include agriculture and forestry operations, urban development, and marinas.

A U.S. law, the Marine Plastic Pollution Research and Control Act of 1987, was passed to implement an international treaty known as MARPOL. Officially the International Convention for the Prevention of Pollution from Ships, the treaty was adopted in 1973 to address marine safety issues and oil pollution from ships. In 1978, MARPOL was expanded to prevent ocean pollution caused by the disposal of various kinds of waste. The treaty is divided into annexes, or sections, and Annex 5 specifically bans the disposal of plastics, including garbage bags, fishing nets, and ropes, into the sea.

The U.S. law that implements MARPOL and Annex 5 also includes a provision that forbids dumping plastic waste within 200 miles (320 km) of the U.S. coast. Within 12 miles (19.2 km) of shore, the dumping of other waste, such as metal and glass, is also prohibited.

In July 1991, another provision of the MARPOL treaty designated the Gulf of Mexico as a Special Area. Since the Gulf is nearly enclosed by land, trash concentrates in the area. With the special designation, no dumping of any kind will be allowed in the Gulf.[3]

OFFSHORE POLLUTANTS

In spite of bans on ocean dumping, hazardous wastes from manufacturing plants, oil refineries, chemical companies, and businesses have been discharged directly into oceans or into streams and rivers that flow into oceans. Rain and melting snow runoff from cities also have carried toxic chemicals into oceans.

Fertilizers and untreated sewage that overflows from waste water treatment plants during rainstorms run off into the seas as well. These "natural pollutants" contain nitrogen and phosphorous that plants and animals need for growth. But excess amounts of such nutrients lead to the rapid growth of aquatic plants called algae. The plants can double in concentration every twenty hours and can stretch for miles.

Algae blooms, as they are known, may be 10 to

13 feet (3–4 m) wide and block sunlight that other aquatic plants need for survival. Algae also absorb oxygen and coat fish with slime, suffocating them. Some types of algae produce a poison that kills fish. Massive fish kills resulting from algae have occurred in coastal waters from Japan to South America to northern Europe.

In the United States, offshore ocean pollution has been widely publicized, especially after medical wastes, untreated sewage, and other dangerous debris washed up on beaches during the summers of 1987, 1988, and 1989. Scores of beaches along the East Coast and along the coasts of Florida and California were closed, and people were advised not to swim because of health risks.

During the past decade, there also have been numerous warnings about the dangers of catching fish and harvesting shellfish off U.S. coasts. Frequently, shellfish beds in the bays along the Atlantic coast and in the Gulf of Mexico are closed because of contamination. Much of the contamination is blamed on the practice of dumping sewage sludge into offshore waters and the overflow of raw sewage from waste water treatment plants that occurs during rainstorms. Sewage often contains traces of toxic pollutants such as PCBs and lead from industrial sources.

The New York–New Jersey coast has been called one of the most contaminated in the nation, partly because 2,600 barge loads of sludge from New York and New Jersey cities were dumped directly into the ocean each year. This practice was banned in New Jersey in 1991 and in New York in 1992.

Even though wastes continue to wash up on shores along U.S. coasts, some improvements have been made, according to the EPA. For one thing, the amount of medical wastes washing ashore has diminished. EPA and state health officials have been able to track and find the sources of medical debris and stop disposal in the ocean.[4]

Yet other kinds of hazardous waste continue to show up on America's shores as fishing crews off the Atlantic coast can attest. It was a common practice before international and federal laws banned most ocean dumping to dispose of barrels of hazardous chemical wastes in the sea. In recent years, fishermen who sail from Gloucester, Massachusetts, have reported an increase in the number of drums of hazardous waste getting caught in fishing nets that drag the Atlantic sea waters.

A captain of one trawler has brought up so many barrels that he can tell whether the material inside is toxic just by color. "If it's yellow, it's okay. If it's blue, you throw it back overboard quickly. I got some purple stuff that spilled on a catch and it curled up the fish," the captain told a *Boston Globe* reporter.[5]

In an incident reported by the *Globe* in February 1991, the crew of the *Vito C*, fishing 120 miles (192 km) off the Massachusetts coast, brought up a net with a barrel of toxic waste that landed on the deck, breaking open. Four men on the vessel were splashed with unidentified toxic chemicals, were overcome by the fumes, and were hospitalized after they returned to shore.

Barrels of hazardous waste materials also have washed up on the shores of other nations. In 1988, Lebanese fishermen pulled up drums of waste from the port of Tyre, and other barrels washed up on the Mediterranean shore north of Beirut. Apparently, the barrels were part of several shipments of hazardous waste from Italy disguised as raw materials or recycling goods.[6]

Toxic substances also were found in drums that washed ashore near Turkish towns on the Black Sea. When the barrels first appeared, town residents emptied them and used them to store food and water. Some people became sick or suffered skin rashes, and a cow that licked the contents of one barrel died within twelve hours. Turkish authorities closed the beaches and collected the barrels, storing them in warehouses or burying them in the sand.

Documents inside some of the barrels showed that they came from Italy, and investigations revealed that the hazardous materials first were shipped to Romania and stored in airport hangars for about a year. No one knows how or when the barrels of waste were dumped into the Black Sea, but articles in French and English newspapers reported that evidence showed the dumping was intentional. Holes were punched in some barrels to make them sink, and those that washed ashore are assumed to be only a small percentage of the total dumped into the sea.[7]

OIL WASTES

Waste materials from oil refineries and spills from oil tankers and drilling rigs account for another kind of dumping practice that contaminates offshore areas around the world. Oil wastes are extremely toxic to aquatic life, and the environmental damage from oil spills has been widely publicized. A notorious example is the 1989 accident of the oil tanker *Exxon Valdez* that spilled nearly 11 million gallons (42 million liters) of oil in Alaska's Prince William Sound.

Exxon, the oil company that owns the tanker, is liable for the costs of cleanup operations that have been going on since the spill. The company claims that the waters and offshore areas have recovered, but a recent federal study of the area shows that it will take years for populations of birds, fish, and other marine life to be restored to what they were before the oil spill. A report in *Greenpeace* noted:

> More wildlife was damaged and killed in this spill than in any other known industrial accident. Seals were brain damaged. Fish larvae were mutated. . . . Some 5,500 sea otters died, and more continue to die from eating contaminated shellfish. Some 22 out of 122 killer whales living in the sound perished. There is widespread damage to kelp forests, an important source of food for marine life, and to other plants in tidal zones along 1,200 miles [1,920 km] of the western boundary of the sound and down into the Gulf of Alaska. Traces of oil derivatives were found in the gallbladders of pollock [fish] up to 600 miles [960 km] away.[8]

MEDITERRANEAN MUCK

Tanker accidents and refinery wastes, along with toxic waste dumping and agricultural runoff, have polluted much of the Mediterranean Sea. Fish, shellfish, and other aquatic life are contaminated with heavy metals, pesticides, and other toxic substances.

Although international agreements have helped reduce the hazardous waste dumped into the sea, tons of toxic materials still end up in the Mediterranean each year. So it is not surprising that in the fall of 1990 more than one hundred dead dolphins washed up on the eastern coast of Spain, apparently killed by a virus. Although a dozen or more aged or sick dolphins are found on Spanish beaches each year, the unusually high number of dolphin deaths in 1990 was linked to toxins. Autopsies revealed extremely high levels of PCBs in the dead dolphins.

Biologists and ecologists theorized that the dolphins ate fish contaminated with PCBs, which in turn weakened the dolphins' immune systems and made them vulnerable to disease. Scientists also suspected that PCBs affected the reproductive systems of dolphins and reduced their numbers even further. A University of Barcelona biologist estimated that as many as ten thousand dolphins were victims of PCB contamination.[9]

THE NASTY NORTH SEA

One of the world's most polluted saltwater bodies is the North Sea, sometimes labeled a "chemical sewer" or "cesspool." Surrounding countries, which include Britain, the Netherlands, Germany, Norway, and Sweden, have dumped toxic wastes into the sea for decades. Several extremely polluted rivers, such as the Rhine, flow into the sea also. Added to the chemical mix is agricultural runoff.

Like the dead dolphins on Spain's Mediterranean shore, dead seals washed up on Germany's North Sea coast, apparently infected by a virus in the polluted waters. In addition, there have been massive fish kills because of algae growth, a result of fertilizer runoff from Norwegian farms.

In 1972, the North Sea nations signed the Oslo Convention to restrict or halt dumping of hazardous industrial waste into the sea. The nations set deadlines for bans on waste dumping, pledging to halt all dumping of industrial waste into the North Sea by January 1, 1990. But Britain, known as the "dirty man of Europe," did not comply and postponed its dumping ban to the end of the decade.

When representatives of the North Sea nations met again in March 1990 for a two-day conference on the environment, some countries were highly critical of Great Britain for continuing to allow waste dumping. Although the amount of industrial waste dumped into the North Sea dropped from 3 million tons (2.7 million tonnes) to 200,000 tons (180,000 tonnes), the Dutch minister of transport pointed a finger at Britain by saying "we all know where those 200,000 tons come from."

According to news reports, British businesses have opposed a ban on ocean dumping because of the cost to convert to land-based disposal or to refurbish factories in order to reduce the amount of hazardous waste produced. But British officials say they are completing as rapidly as possible new facilities for waste disposal so that ocean dumping can be halted.[10]

CONTAMINATION IN THE IRISH SEA

British facilities also are contaminating areas of the Irish Sea, near Wales. The British Nuclear Fuels reprocessing plant, located at Sellafield on the North Wales coast, discharges 2 million gallons (7.6 million liters) of radioactive water into the sea every day.

The radioactive materials include plutonium, a highly radioactive by-product of nuclear reactors. Plutonium is used in the manufacture of nuclear weapons.

Activists have been calling for an end to imports of nuclear wastes for reprocessing. The plant accepts radioactive waste not only from the United Kingdom but also from other countries with nuclear reactors, such as France and Japan.

A 1990 study of the area by British officials disclosed high levels of plutonium contamination in coastal sediments from several locations along the Wales coast, from the Dee Estuary (a northern inlet) to the Lleyn Peninsula. At the Dee Estuary, officials found levels of plutonium one hundred times higher than those found near Chernobyl, a nuclear plant in the Soviet Ukraine that exploded in 1986. The Chernobyl accident spewed radioactive materials over large areas of Europe and left several dozen people dead and many others with possible health problems caused by radiation. The total contamination from radioactive materials in the coastal region of the Irish Sea, however, is much less than that of the Chernobyl area.[11]

7 Military Dumping

Along with industry and agriculture, the military dumps vast amounts of hazardous materials into the oceans and on land in many parts of the world. In the United States, some military bases are the most hazardous waste sites in the nation, and U.S. military bases abroad have been responsible for severe contamination of soil and waterways, particularly in Europe and in South Pacific island nations. In addition, the United States and other nuclear powers have tested their bombs and other munitions in the oceans or on islands, destroying aquatic and land-based plant and animal life.

TOXIC WASTE AT U.S. MILITARY BASES

When the U.S. Congress passed the Resource Conservation and Recovery Act (RCRA), the federal law was designed in part to prevent environmental damage from hazardous waste. The law, however, has applied only to private businesses and local governments in the United States, even though provisions of

RCRA require federal agencies and facilities to comply with regulations for hazardous and other waste disposal. Federal courts have ruled that U.S. operations are exempt from civil fines for violations of RCRA and other environmental laws. Because of these rulings, Congress passed the Federal Facility Compliance Act of 1991, which allows the EPA to enforce waste-management laws and gives states the power to impose penalties for violations at federal facilities.

Military bases, which are under the authority of the U.S. Department of Defense (DOD), and nuclear weapons facilities, which are controlled by the Department of Energy (DOE), are responsible for thousands of contaminated sites in the United States and overseas. Some of the most polluted are nuclear weapons plants. Huge amounts of solvents, heavy metals, PCBs, asbestos, battery acids, pesticides, and almost every other kind of toxic substance have polluted areas in every state in the nation. The toxic pollutants cause cancer, birth defects, and liver diseases as well as other serious health problems.

According to a report in *Newsweek*, "The military's 871 domestic installations, strung across 25 million acres of land, produce more tons of hazardous waste each year than the top five U.S. chemical companies combined. Department of Defense reports document 8,000 sites that may require some form of environmental restoration, a task that could take 20 years and $20 billion, or more."[1]

But a seven-year study by the Military Toxics Network revealed a much higher number of contaminated U.S. military sites. When installations in Washington, D.C., Puerto Rico, Guam, and the Trust

Territories are included, there are 14,401 contaminated sites on 1,579 military bases, the organization noted in its report published in 1991.[2]

Wastes from nuclear weapons and power plants also add to the total number of federal facilities that are contaminated as well as to the costs for cleanup. In a series titled "Toxic Waste: A Federal Failure," in the *Los Angeles Times*, one report said costs of hazardous-waste cleanup could be as high as $500 billion, and some sites may never be cleaned because the price tag is too high. The nuclear weapons complex in Hanford, Washington, for example, is so contaminated that it could cost $40 billion for cleanup. At that price, the DOE might opt instead to seal off the complex as a "national sacrifice zone."[3]

Since the military has kept most of its operations secret, claiming "national security" as the reason, Americans know little about the hazards that defense operations pose to the U.S. environment and public health. Until recently, citizens groups have not been allowed to check on military operations. But a number of investigative reports, including one by the Office of Technology Assessment, which advises Congress on technology, have shown that the U.S. military is by far the nation's worst polluter and has exposed thousands of Americans and citizens in other parts of the world to deadly chemicals and radioactivity.

Another factor that has helped bring to light contamination at military bases is budget cuts. The Defense Department plans to close dozens of military bases in the United States and abroad. Before any of the bases can be sold to civilians or local government agencies, the DOD is required by law to decontaminate the sites. That means extensive cleanup efforts will be required at overseas operations as well as at U.S. bases.

TOXIC TRAIL ABROAD

The extent of contamination from U.S. military bases overseas is not well known because the military has just begun to examine the situation. News reporters for the *Los Angeles Times* based their stories on interviews with U.S. and European military officers and U.S. Defense Department documents. Under the Freedom of Information Act, government agencies must supply data requested by citizens unless the information would threaten national security. Investigations revealed situations such as these:

- U.S. Air Force bases in Germany—the Rhine-Main base near Frankfort and the Bitburg base—have polluted soil and groundwater. Jet fuel leaked from underground tanks and pipelines at Rhine-Main, and cleanup is expected to take five years at a cost of $15 million. At Bitburg, an inadequate sewage treatment plant has polluted the Kyll River and other streams with organic waste and toxic chemicals.
- Toxic solvents (used to clean trucks and tanks) and leaking oil tanks at U.S. Army depot stations at Mannheim, Germersheim, and Mainz have contaminated underground water supplies.
- Unlined landfills at other U.S. bases in Germany

contain a variety of hazardous wastes that are expected to contaminate the surrounding soil and waterways.

Defense Department officials told James Broder, a *Times* reporter, that the military followed waste disposal practices commonly accepted in the past. These included dumping oils and solvents on the ground or into tanks buried underground and dumping wastes into unlined pits or waterways. Officials noted, however, that military officers are "a lot more sensitive" to environmental issues today than past commanders were. They also are aware that environmental pollution creates foreign policy problems. The United States cannot maintain good relations with a country if it pulls out troops and turns over contaminated military bases to the host nations.[4]

In some areas of the world, citizen groups are speaking out against U.S. bases in their countries, staging protests over environmental and health hazards. A coalition of Japanese organizations has gone beyond protest to file a lawsuit in a U.S. district court in Washington, D.C. against the U.S. Navy. The coalition charges the navy with failure to consider the environmental impacts of its operations at its base in Yokosuka, Japan, and at its nearby airport.

Earlier, the Japanese coalition had petitioned the U.S. Navy to provide relief from noise levels many times greater than those considered safe by the EPA. These noises occur every few minutes daily between 8 A.M. and 10 P.M. In addition, the suit charges that the navy is destroying a forest to build housing and other facilities for navy personnel, is engaged in destructive dredging in Tokyo Bay, and is releasing massive amounts of hazardous waste into the bay and surrounding land areas.

"The Navy seems to think that the people of Japan are not entitled to the same basic environmental protection which the Navy would clearly be required to provide were these facilities located within the United States," a U.S. attorney for the plaintiffs said.[5]

POISONS IN THE PACIFIC

For almost three decades, the French have been conducting nuclear tests on two small islands in French Polynesia. Well after the Americans, British, and Soviets agreed in 1963 to ban nuclear tests in the area, the French selected an atomic test site on the Moruroa atoll. In 1966, a bomb was placed on a barge in a lagoon. "When it was detonated, all the water in the shallow lagoon basin was sucked up into the air, and then rained down. The islets on the encircling reef were all covered with heaps of irradiated fish and clams, whose slowly rotting flesh continued to stink for weeks," wrote Bengt Danielsson, an anthropologist in Tahiti.

In an article for *The Bulletin of the Atomic Scientists*, Danielsson explained that in spite of many protests from the Polynesian people, the French continued atomic tests. Over the next eight years another forty-four bombs, including five hydrogen bombs, were exploded in the atmosphere over Moruroa and Fangataufa, another small island.[6]

Although the Polynesian protests were not heeded, the French could not ignore the outcry from nearby nations that suffered from radioactive fallout. As atmospheric testing continued, Australia, New Zealand, and other Pacific nations organized a boycott against the French, refusing to buy French goods or use French transportation services. Australia and New Zealand also initiated a lawsuit against France. These actions stopped the blasts in the skies but not the tests. The French set up underground testing sites on Moruroa. Over the years, bombs have blasted the island, crumbling its base and causing it to subside nearly 5 feet (1.5 m).[7]

Radioactive material has leaked into the ocean, and nuclear waste has been dumped into the waters near the Polynesian islands. Several cyclones during the 1980s also have carried nuclear wastes over the area. But no one knows the extent of contamination because the French have never allowed independent scientists more than a few days to investigate.

When Greenpeace activists were in New Zealand in 1985 to protest continued nuclear testing in French Polynesia, French secret service agents attached mines to the hull of the Greenpeace ship *Rainbow Warrior* while it was docked. The ensuing explosion killed a photographer aboard. Two French agents were captured in New Zealand and convicted of manslaughter. But six years later, in Paris, one of the agents was given the Order of Merit and made a French knight. New Zealand's foreign affairs minister sent a protest letter to the French ambassador, and Greenpeace condemned the award, challenging the bomber to show his medal to the children of the photographer who died in the blast.

The French government also has blocked studies by impartial health experts who have tried to gather statistics about the incidence of cancer among Polynesians. French officials say that one independent study showed no increase in cancer rates over the past few decades, but the study was not conducted by health professionals. Medical experts investigating other South Pacific islands, where the United States and Britain conducted atomic tests during the late 1950s, believe there are a growing number of people with cancers caused by radiation fallout.

Nuclear tests, along with other military activities such as construction projects on coral reefs, have caused additional health problems in the South Pacific. Damaged coral leads to a poisoning of fish with a toxin known as ciguatera. Tilman Ruff, an Australian expert in preventive medicine, explained:

> Small, single-celled marine organisms found in coral reefs produce ciguatera toxins. When coral is destroyed or damaged, either the number of these toxic organisms increases, or the damage encourages the organisms to produce higher levels of toxins. Plant-eating fish that inhabit the reefs eat these toxic organisms and in turn are eaten by larger, carnivorous fish. The toxins have no observable effect on the fish, but when humans catch and consume them, ciguatera poisoning ensues.[8]

Symptoms of the poisoning range from diarrhea to paralysis, and some people suffer from effects of the disease for weeks or many months. Although outbreaks of the disease have been traced to reef damage caused by storms or earthquakes, frequently damage is the result of military operations in the area.

Other threats to public health and the environment are posed by a chemical weapons dump in the

South Pacific. Since 1971, the U.S. Army has stored dangerous chemical compounds on the Johnston Atoll, a tiny island southwest of Honolulu. The compounds include Agent Orange, a deadly dioxin herbicide used to destroy foliage during the Vietnam War, and nerve gases. In late 1990, obsolete chemical weapons from U.S. bases in Germany also were shipped to the atoll. The United States plans to burn the chemicals in a large-scale incinerator specially built for weapons destruction.

Although the U.S. military claims that the incinerator destroys chemicals safely, leaving no contaminants, environmental groups and political leaders of Pacific Island nations adamantly disagree. Critics point to malfunctions of the incinerator in test operations and the fact that military personnel have been forced from the island because of severe storms. Opponents believe that alternative methods, such as using bacteria or light to break down chemicals, can be used. But the army argues that such technology has not been fully developed and could cause unexpected problems. There also are concerns that the deteriorating weapons may leak or explode if they are left in storage too much longer.

Along with storage of chemical weapons, the Johnston Atoll has been the site of U.S. nuclear tests and open burning of Agent Orange. Some areas are dangerously contaminated with radioactivity and dioxin. As a result, the island is considered one of the worst Superfund sites—among the top ten in the United States and its territories—that need cleanup.

Many citizens in Hawaii and on other Pacific islands believe the United States is using the region as a huge dump for extremely hazardous wastes. They fear also that other dangerous activities will go on without public scrutiny. Although many support the destruction of chemical weapons, they also believe that every attempt should be made to conduct these activities with the least amount of risk to the environment and public health.[9]

8 Dumping at the Bottom of the World

Can you imagine a huge pile of refuse on the shores of remote and icy Antarctica where only a few thousand people have ever lived for any length of time? Many people envision the Antarctic—the South Pole—as a "pure" continent, about 5,500,000 square miles (14,300,000 sq km) of ice-covered land free of civilization's problems and pollution. Indeed, it is one of the cleanest places in the world. But when scientists began to investigate Antarctica, beginning in the late 1950s and early 1960s, they generated trash. Over the years garbage has been piling up because it does not decompose in the frigid climate.

THE ANTARCTIC TREATY

The continent is under the jurisdiction of the Antarctic Treaty, which became effective in 1961. Nations that originally signed the treaty (Argentina, Australia, Belgium, Chile, France, Japan, New Zealand, Norway, South Africa, Soviet Union, United Kingdom, and

United States) agreed that Antarctica belongs to the world. They promised to set aside territorial claims and to protect and use the continent for peaceful purposes, particularly scientific research.

Today, twenty-six nations are consultative parties to the treaty. These nations are involved in major scientific research and have research bases in the area. Because of their vested interests, these nations are allowed to vote on matters concerning Antarctica. Another thirteen nations have signed the treaty but have no voting rights.[1]

Although there are forty scientific stations in Antarctica, the human population consists of only a few thousand people who operate and maintain the bases from about November or December through February, the season when the ice melts on coastal areas of the continent. Scientists study Antarctic wildlife, climate patterns, and the "ozone hole," in which chemical reactions deplete the thin layer of ozone gas in the stratosphere. The ozone layer protects the planet from ultraviolet rays of the sun.

THREATS TO THE ANTARCTIC

Over the years, bases have grown in size to accommodate an increasing number of researchers and maintenance staff. For example, the U.S. McMurdo station on the eastern side of Antarctica may be considered a "town," with over a thousand summer residents. Airstrips have been built, and large oil tanks have been brought in to store fuel for heating and to generate electricity.

In addition, several thousand tourists visit Mc-

Murdo and other bases in Antarctica annually. Most tourists arrive on cruise ships from Chile. According to a report in *Time* magazine, "About 3,500 people, mostly Americans, paid $5,000 to $16,000 to sail over from South America [in 1989]. They generally stayed in Antarctica four or five days. . . . So many boats cruise along the peninsula between November and March that it has been dubbed the 'Antarctic Riviera.' Chile has opened a hotel near its base. Antarctic activities include hiking, mountain climbing, dogsledding, camping and skiing." But these activities can disrupt feeding and reproductive patterns of seabirds, and litter left by tourists pollutes the environment. Some visitors have even scratched graffiti on rocks.[2]

In 1986, the environmental organization Greenpeace set up a small base near the U.S. and New Zealand stations to monitor the effects of human activities on the continent. Greenpeace began to publicize its findings: environmental pollution at several stations. At McMurdo, it was common practice to bulldoze tons of solid waste into an open pit, pour thousands of gallons of waste fuel over the refuse and burn it. Ash and residue were later compacted in a landfill. In addition, untreated sewage was pumped into the ocean, and 50,000 gallons (190,000 liters) of oil leaked from tanks, polluting the surrounding area.

Although some stations found the Greenpeace investigations helpful, others claimed that the organization had exaggerated environmental hazards at the South Pole. As polluting activities continued, so did the adverse publicity. In 1990, the Environmental Defense Fund (EDF), an activist organization of U.S. scientists and lawyers working to protect ecosystems worldwide, threatened a lawsuit. The EDF charged that McMurdo was violating federal environmental laws and also international regulations established to protect Antarctica. By 1991, waste disposal practices had changed at the station and other U.S. bases, as well as those operated by a few other nations. Now trash is sorted and recycled or shipped back to the countries from which it came, and dump sites are being cleaned up.[3]

Yet there are some stations that are still a danger to the environment. In 1991, Greenpeace investigated abandoned bases owned by Britain, Chile, and Argentina, and reported:

> At all but one, the expedition found that fuel, batteries and other hazardous materials had been left behind to weather the elements. At the old British facility on Deception Island there were oil drums with perfectly sealed bungs and rusted out bottoms. At Gonzalez Videla, an abandoned Chilean station, Greenpeace pumped oil from rusting barrels into new drums from its polar ship *Gondwana*, and then moved them into a shed for protection.
>
> The most deplorable messes are not limited to abandoned stations. At Arturo Prat, one of the principal operating Chilean stations . . . the Greenpeace expedition crew discovered an area they nicknamed "the field of death." . . . Forty years of abandoned rubbish, burned trash and leaking fuel had turned a once-lush expanse of moss into a muddy morass of oily ash and garbage.

Still, the Greenpeace crew also saw evidence of increased sensitivity to the environment. At an Argentine station, the officer in charge began a cleanup of an old dump in the midst of a penguin colony and told Greenpeace that he would try to obtain a trash compactor so that he could send waste materials back to Argentina.[4]

DEBATES OVER MINING

Efforts to protect Antarctica from hazardous materials have included campaigns to regulate or ban oil and mineral exploration at the South Pole. In 1988, representatives of the signatory nations of the Antarctic Treaty met in Wellington, New Zealand, and drafted an agreement called the Convention on the Regulation of Antarctic Mineral Resource Activities, also known as the Wellington Convention. The accord proposed strict regulations for commercial prospecting and development of resources in Antarctica. Supporters believed that the treaty would prevent exploitation of Antarctica by setting up rigid protective measures and providing an agency to enforce regulations.

Even though the agreement provides for stringent tests to prevent environmental damage, the accord has created controversy and has been widely criticized by environmentalists. Critics say the treaty does not provide any clear goals for the continent, and the very existence of the treaty implies that mining of natural resources in Antarctica is acceptable. Opponents also argue that member nations have not always been concerned about protecting the environment and have given little consideration to the impact of the increasing number of bases in the South Pole region.[5]

Jacques Cousteau, a marine environmentalist known worldwide, has pointed out that mining for natural resources could affect the world's climate by disrupting the vital cooling element—the ice cap. The glacial cap "reflects up to 80 percent of the solar radiation it receives, thereby helping maintain low temperatures in the area. This capacity for 'manufacturing' cold . . . allows regulation of the earth's mean temperature," Cousteau explained in an interview for the *Christian Science Monitor*.[6]

Cousteau and his environmental organization, the Cousteau Society, conducted a worldwide campaign to persuade member nations of the Antarctic Treaty to reject the Wellington Convention. The Cousteau Society was instrumental in gathering millions of signatures on a petition demanding that France establish a policy to protect Antarctica from mining and other industrial activities. France has joined Australia, New Zealand, and other nations in seeking a total ban on exploration of natural resources in the South Pole.[7]

An alliance of some two hundred environmental groups also has aggressively opposed the mining regulations. Critics say the Wellington Convention would open the area to the kinds of hazards that have been created in Alaska's Prince William Sound. Opponents cite an accident that occurred in 1989, when the *Bahia Paraiso*, an Argentine transport ship, ran aground and sank near Palmer Station, a U.S. base at the tip of the Antarctic peninsula.

The *Bahia Paraiso* carried 700 metric tons (about 250,000 gallons [950,000 liters]) of diesel fuel and tanks of compressed propane gas to resupply the Argentine base in Antarctica. In addition, eighty-one tourists, along with a crew of over two hundred, were aboard. All of the tourists and crew were rescued because of quick action by scientists at Palmer Station and by the crew of a cruise ship that happened to be nearby. But leaking fuel, estimated at 3,000 gallons (11,400 liters) a day, caused great environmental damage.[8]

Thousands of krill, a shrimplike animal, and seabirds were killed. Many penguins and other wildlife also were destroyed by the leaking oil. Workers with equipment to contain the spill arrived the next day to begin cleanup operations. But scientists predicted that because of the extreme cold, it would take from fifty to one hundred years for the oil on shore to break down.[9]

PRESSURE FOR A MINING BAN

In the spring of 1991, the Antarctic Treaty nations began negotiating a treaty that included a fifty-year ban on mining in Antarctica. All signatory nations would have to approve a repeal of the ban. The draft treaty also contained a provision to designate the continent as a "World Park," or wilderness area.

Delegates from signatory nations met in Madrid, Spain, in June to sign the accord. During the convention, U.S. delegates demanded that the treaty include a clause giving the United States the right to withdraw from the agreement if a few countries voted against a change. As a result, the treaty was rewritten and the draft again presented to delegates for approval. All nations had to approve the treaty in order for it to become effective. However, the day before the signing ceremony, the United States asked for more time to study the proposal.

The U.S. action brought sharp criticism from other Atlantic Treaty delegates. Editorials in some major U.S. newspapers were also highly critical. *The New*

York Times, for example, called President George Bush's environmental policy "Blind on Antarctica."[10] The prime minister of Australia and legislators from European nations and Japan wrote to Bush urging him to support the mining ban.

Then on July 4, 1991, President Bush did an about-face. He announced that the United States would sign the international agreement to ban international mining in Antarctica and preserve the continent. The treaty prohibits oil drilling and mineral exploration for fifty years. At the end of that time, another agreement will have to be enacted. To repeal the ban, three-fourths of the treaty nations with voting rights would have to agree to such a measure.

Some environmentalists were concerned that the three-fourths vote required to repeal the mining ban would allow countries to disregard a commitment to preserve Antarctica. But others are hopeful that President Bush's promise, delivered during his July 4 announcement, will hold true: "The new environmental measures will protect native species of antarctic flora and fauna and will place needed limits on tourism, waste disposal and marine pollution."[11]

Debris and Nuclear Hazards in Space

No land or sea area on earth seems to be off limits to global garbage, hazardous waste, or toxic products. Within the past few decades, even outer space has become a depository for trash, a great garbage dump in orbit. More than 6.5 million pounds of debris from manufactured items (as opposed to natural cosmic debris like interplanetary dust particles and meteorites) streak around the planet, endangering spacecraft and astronauts in flight.[1]

Radioactive satellites also threaten astronauts in space and are a danger to the global environment if they accidentally plunge back to Earth. In addition, scientists report that nuclear-powered spacecraft release radioactive materials that can disrupt the operation of satellites.

SPACE JUNK

Since 1957, when the Soviet Union launched Sputnik I and the United States followed with its satellite, debris in space has been accumulating at a rapid rate. In 1961, the U.S. Air Force was able to track by ground radar only sixty objects orbiting the planet. But five years later, researchers estimated that 1,300 objects measuring 10 centimeters (nearly 4 inches) or more were in near-Earth orbit.[2]

Today the U.S. Space Surveillance Network is tracking over 6,600 artificial objects larger than a softball. About 6 percent are operating satellites, but the other items are junk. Scientists estimate that 3.5 million bits of debris may be part of the junkyard in earth orbit. The orbiting trash includes fragments of metal, paint, and other materials, such as nuclear fuel from spacecraft reactors. Some particles are no larger than a grain of salt or the period at the end of this sentence.

Fragments and larger pieces of debris come from satellites that have exploded accidentally or have been blown up intentionally to protect secret technology. Others are parts of spent rockets or launchers. Still other objects were lost by astronauts working in space—screwdrivers, nuts, bolts, and even a thermal glove or two.

HAZARDS OF ORBITING TRASH

Why are these objects, especially tiny flakes and fragments, hazardous? At blinding speeds, from about 15,000 to over 30,000 miles (24,000–48,000 km) per hour, debris may hit spacecraft with tremendous force. Particles of paint that flake from spacecraft, for example, travel at 15,639 miles (25,022 km) per hour. This is comparable to driving from San Francisco to New York in just ten minutes—if that were possible.[3]

At such speed, the destructive energy is tremendous. Suppose an object weighing 1/35 that of an aspirin tablet travels at 10 kilometers a second (6 miles per second or 360 miles per minute). On impact, it would have the force of a shotgun pellet, according to scientists who study space debris.[4]

A tiny paint chip less than .01 inch (.025 cm) in diameter put a pit in the window of the *Challenger* spacecraft traveling in Earth orbit during a 1983 mission. The windshield had to be replaced at a cost of $50,000. The following year, a satellite was disabled because of bombarding fragments. Thousands of tiny particles of space junk, which included microscopic specks of human urine, smashed into the satellite, according to scientists who analyzed it later.[5]

In January 1990, the space shuttle *Columbia* returned to Earth with a captured satellite called the Long Duration Exposure Facility (LDEF). About the size of a school bus, the LDEF had been in space for almost six years, although its planned stay was only ten months. Space activity came to a halt for several years after the *Challenger* exploded minutes after liftoff in 1986. The LDEF carried several dozen experiments, but it returned with unexpected data for scientists. It was pockmarked with up to forty thousand holes per square meter.

Fragments of natural and artificial debris struck the satellite at speeds of 10 to 70 kilometers per second (6 to 43 miles per second). By studying the captured satellite, scientists will try to determine the hazards posed by space debris and how best to protect satellites, spacecraft, and other space equipment, as well as astronauts, from collisions.[6]

Astronauts have not been endangered by space

junk, but scientists believe that as space debris increases, so will the hazards. A 1990 report from the U.S. Office of Technology Assessment pointed out that a paint chip could puncture the pressurized suit of an astronaut walking in space. A University of Illinois scientist fears that a piece of space junk could pierce a spacecraft and destroy it, which would be fatal for the astronauts.[7]

Collisions of space debris with spacecraft or satellites are expected to be more likely in the years ahead. In fact, scientists believe that there is a good chance (one in one hundred) that the $1.5 billion Hubble Space Telescope launched in 1990 could be severely damaged by space debris during its seventeen-year life span.

Although the rate of space activity has remained fairly constant since 1965, space debris increases because of collisions. A collision causes a spray of millions of tiny specks or pieces, far more than would occur with an explosion. The debris created can start a chain reaction with ever more collisions and junk fragments orbiting in space. The OTA and other experts predict that space exploration and travel could become too risky to attempt if space activity increases and junk accumulates at a more rapid rate in near-Earth orbits.[8]

PROTECTION FROM SPACE DEBRIS

Is anything being done to protect space structures and the people in them from the hazards of orbiting trash? Spacecraft have been protected with aluminum shields, but these have added to the space junk problem. When debris hits the bumper, a spray of aluminum fragments from the shield spews into orbit. Researchers have experimented with other materials and have found that several thin layers of ceramic fabric may absorb the impact of any oncoming fragments, allowing them to shatter in stages and release less debris. Such shields may be installed on all space structures.

Space structures also have been designed so that ground controllers can maneuver them out of the path of oncoming junk being tracked by radar. There also could be onboard control systems that work in a similar fashion.

National Aeronautics and Space Administration (NASA) researchers are especially concerned about protecting the space station *Freedom*, which may be launched by the year 2000. The station will be the largest structure ever placed in orbit and will include modules to house a crew of eight. These modules will be protected by shields, and the entire space station will be maneuvered out of the path of oncoming debris if radar shows that a collision is imminent.

Another protective measure is the development of a space telescope that would allow astronauts to detect debris far away and trigger a radar system that would tell astronauts how much time they have to take defensive action. The telescope is being designed by researchers at NASA's Johnson Space Center in Houston, Texas.

Sensors in the telescope will record objects in sunlight and darkness. Since particles moving in space emit heat, they can be detected by infrared sensors. Data will help scientists determine the size and speed of particles. Such information may lead to protection from debris not only for the space station but also for important satellites.

For the past decade, space scientists also have been researching methods to clean up space debris or to prevent its accumulation. In some cases, space structures may be maneuvered to low orbits so that they drop back to Earth's atmosphere and burn up. Launches of spacecraft may also be planned so that nonessential items, such as upper stages of rockets, would burn up in the atmosphere and not orbit. Ground controllers may send nonoperative satellites to higher orbits and park them there. Scientists also are experimenting with a robotic structure that could scoop up tons of debris from space and remove it to lower orbits, where it would eventually drop into Earth's atmosphere, or to higher orbits where there is less traffic.

NUCLEAR REACTORS IN SPACE

One of the serious hazards posed by space debris is the possibility of colliding with nuclear-powered space structures, causing them to fall back to Earth. Spacecraft that operate on nuclear energy carry highly radioactive materials.

"There are two fundamental sources of nuclear power for applications in space: reactors and radioisotope power supplies. Whereas a reactor produces heat through the controlled fission of uranium fuel, a radioisotope thermoelectric generator, or RTG, derives heat simply from the decay of a highly radioactive material. In both cases, the heat is converted to electric power," according to a report published in *Scientific American*.

The U.S. and Soviet scientists who wrote the report pointed out that the United States launched its first and only RTG satellite in 1965; it operated forty-three days and is still in orbit. Between 1970 and 1988, the Soviets sent thirty-one RTG satellites into space to monitor U.S. Navy activities; none have been launched since them. "The jettisoned reactors from 29 of these systems are still in orbit, along with hundreds of kilograms of radioactive fuel," the scientists noted.[9]

The hazardous reactors have been maneuvered to so-called storage orbits, where they travel for several hundred years, allowing decay of radioactive materials until they are safe for reentry into earth's atmosphere. But two Soviet reactors fell back to Earth accidentally. One was *Cosmos 954*, which crashed in 1978 in northwestern Canada and spewed radioactive debris over thousands of square miles. Collecting the debris and decontaminating the site cost the Canadian government about $10 million. Another accident caused the breakup of a satellite over Alaska in 1984. Some scientists have speculated that the accidents might have been caused by collisions with space debris.[10]

Whether or not collisions have occurred, the nuclear-powered craft still in space are orbiting in areas full of junk. Thus, as the debris increases, there is greater possibility of an accident. In addition, nuclear power reactors will fall back to Earth eventually and could contaminate the environment with radioactive materials.

Space scientists emphasize that planetary explorations depend on nuclear power and that radioactive hazards for Earth diminish or disappear when nuclear-powered spacecraft soar to other planets. But nuclear power systems in near-Earth orbit pose significant dangers, and scientists suggest that an international treaty be drawn up to guard against radioactive contamination on Earth. An agreement would ban nuclear power sources from lower orbits and allow their use only for deep-space applications.

10 Global Cleanup and Protection?

Controlling global garbage and hazardous waste and debris certainly requires international cooperation. But national governments also must develop policies that protect the earth's natural resources from toxic materials and take into account impacts on the global community, not just "home base." In addition, citizens working individually or collectively have to act to prevent environmental and health hazards from toxic materials.

INTERNATIONAL COOPERATION

In June 1992, a United Nations Conference on Environment and Development (UNCED) was held in Rio de Janeiro, Brazil. Known as "Eco 92" or the "Earth Summit," the conference marked the twentieth anniversary of the first U.N. conference on the environment, which took place in Stockholm, Sweden. At the time of the Stockholm conference, pollution was highly visible in many industrialized nations. Smog, foul waterways, and mountains of garbage and trash were just some of the contaminants people had to combat.

Although some progress has been made in the struggle to protect the environment in the United States and other countries, governments and citizens have become aware of the interrelated nature of pollution problems, whether local, national, or global in scale. The issues of climate change brought on by the greenhouse effect, depletion of the protective ozone layer in the stratosphere, and trade in hazardous waste and products exemplify how human activities can have a global impact. These issues were at the top of the agenda for the 1992 UN conference.

During 1990 and 1991, in preparation for the conference, representatives from national governments and nongovernmental organizations contributed ideas, submitted scientific studies, and developed strategies for environmental improvements. Frequently, participants called for industrialized nations to set standards for a "sustainable" environment—that is, policies that allow renewal and restoration of natural resources. There was also criticism of countries such as the United States that have achieved economic success at the expense of the global environment and poor nations.

Ricardo Bayon, who edits a newsletter published by the Centre for Our Common Future at the United Nations, explained:

> Any discussion dealing with the environment in developing countries necessarily runs into one barrier that has yet to be cleared: the differences between environmentalism in the North (the developed countries) and the South (the underdeveloped countries). . . . This is nothing new. In the first World Conference on the

> Environment, held in 1972 . . . the countries from the South refused to address the environment because they were more concerned with development. They said the North's concern with the environment was a farce.
>
> Since then, the tune has been changing slightly, and that, in itself, [is] a sign of hope, because to consider development without taking into account the environment is also a farce. Hence the validity of a term such as sustainable development which stresses progress that can be maintained, development that does not undermine our children's ability to develop.[1]

Sustainable development was one of the major environmental policies outlined in the *U.S. Report* submitted to the 1992 conference. Written by members of the Council on Environmental Quality, the report analyzes global trends and environmental problems and suggests solutions.

The *U.S. Report* calls attention to the need for cooperation with other nations to "manage natural resources in a sustainable fashion" and at the same time "promote international trade and economic development." Other trends in U.S. environmental policies are noted, such as alliances formed in the United States between government, private companies, and environmental groups to solve pollution problems. Vigorous enforcement of environmental laws and ways to prevent pollution are emphasized in the report as well.

PROBLEMS WITH POLLUTION CONTROL

In the United States, federal law requires manufacturers and businesses to disclose what kinds of toxic chemicals are being stored or used in their facilities. Because of the "right-to-know" law, people are able to obtain information about hazardous materials to which they may be exposed. This has helped communities and activist groups pressure industries to reduce releases of hazardous materials.

Companies may be forced by law to take corrective action if they contaminate the environment. Usually, firms must develop technologies for cleanup or install expensive equipment to control waste.

"The amount spent on pollution control has increased approximately four-fold from 1972–1990," according to the Council on Environmental Quality. "This rise in spending coincides with a rise in the extent of environmental regulation. The U.S. Code of Federal Regulations contained 2,763 pages on 'Protection of the Environment,' in 1975. In 1990, the same section of the U.S. Code contained 11,087 pages."[2]

Environmental laws and public pressure to enforce them have helped restore some extremely polluted areas in the United States. But enforcing tough regulations does not always bring the desired results. For example, EPA regulations set up under the Superfund law require industries to pay the major share of costs to clean up municipal landfills where toxic waste has been dumped. Before the dangers of this kind of dumping were understood, industries regularly used municipal landfills for hazardous waste disposal. But household garbage, trash from schools and small businesses, and other wastes were also dumped in the landfills.

EPA regulations allow corporations to find and sue other waste generators for their share of cleanup costs, which average about $30 million for each hazardous waste site. As a result, companies have initiated lawsuits against towns, school districts, small businesses (like restaurants), scrap yards, nursing homes, and sometimes even banks and real estate firms that have arranged loans for contaminated property. In several cases brought against large corporations, hundreds of smaller parties have been sued. Environmentalists, city officials, those who wrote the Superfund act, and many others claim that corporations are trying to undermine provisions of the law that set liabilities for waste disposal. Corporations, on the other hand, believe they are being unfairly singled out to pay huge sums for hazardous-waste cleanup.[3]

TOWARD "CLEAN TECHNOLOGIES"

As lawsuits stall cleanup and add to the costs, experts in toxic-waste reduction have urged the nation to balance the regulatory policies with more positive incentives for waste reduction. In 1990, Congress passed the Pollution Prevention Act, which emphasizes waste reduction at its source rather than just controlling pollutants. This means adopting a safe-materials and clean-technologies approach to managing hazardous materials.

Such a strategy has been encouraged in Europe in recent years. The Dutch, for example, have established a Department for Clean Technologies, which provides funds for research and demonstration projects. In Switzerland, Product Life Institute, a new research center, offers studies for developing products so that they will last longer and reduce the use of resources, waste, and energy consumption. In Germany, new industries are required by federal law to use the most recent technology to reduce or recycle wastes.

In the United States, laws have been passed in a

number of states requiring industries to reduce the use of toxic materials. The Toxics Use Reduction Institute at the University of Lowell in Massachusetts has been set up to help obtain such objectives. According to Ken Geiser, director of the institute, "The full life cycle of a material from development through use to disposal must be planned and accounted for in the true cost of a product. Social and environmental effects must be factored into corporate decisions about material use and product production. New chemicals or new processes must be evaluated in terms of caution and conservation, rather than risk and expediency."

Geiser explained that "toxics use reduction differs from the conventional government approach regulating the management of waste by moving the policy focus directly into the industrial production process . . . programs require firms to identify the most toxic chemicals they use and develop plans for how they will reduce the use of those substances in the future," thus generating less hazardous waste and creating safer workplaces.[4]

Similar ideas were described by Bruce Piasecki and Peter Asmus in their book *In Search of Environmental Excellence*. The authors called the concept a "new industrial design triangle" that makes economic and environmental goals compatible and that is based on three principles: conserving energy, saving materials, and reducing waste. They cited a number of examples of how the concept is being applied by U.S. companies.

In California, the state's health department, a waste-recovery company, and a manufacturer of circuit boards worked together to develop a method to turn heavy metal waste from the production of circuit boards into solid metallic sheets that are sold as scrap. The toxic metal does not go into the waste stream, and the scrap metal is recycled to make new materials. "The system can save a firm upward of $100,000 in legal bills alone, and can speed up business operations by eliminating the need for lengthy state or federal regulatory review," wrote Piasecki and Asmus.[5]

Many companies are beginning to look at the increasing expenses associated with toxic waste and are finding recovering or recycling materials can be cost-effective. For example, chemical companies, which have a notorious record of pollution, are finding that they can alter their manufacturing processes to be more efficient and at the same time produce less waste. Du Pont, for one, discovered that it could reduce toxic waste in a paint and plastics plant the company operates in Beaumont, Texas. At first, engineers argued that reducing pollution would be too expensive, but they came to the opposite conclusion after changing the production process. By using less of one raw material, they were able to cut hazardous waste by two-thirds. As costs went down, yields increased, saving the company $1 million a year, according to a report in *The Wall Street Journal*.[6]

At 3M Company, engineers are reformulating products so that hazardous materials are not used. Since the 1970s, 3M has been reducing pollution and has saved nearly $500 million. The company hopes to cut hazardous pollutants by 90 percent before the end of the 1990s.[7]

In Europe, some companies are finding ways to reduce the amount of packaging that enters the waste stream. Many packaging containers are made of plastic materials that generate toxins when manufactured. But waste-reduction policies in Europe are geared toward conservation—using refillable containers and placing a tax on throwaways. For example, in Denmark, the government bans all nonrefillable containers. In Norway, the government places a tax of 3.5 kronens (50 cents) on each nonreturnable beverage bottle or can. As a result, Norwegians use 35 percent more returnables than throwaway containers.[8]

CHANGING CONSUMER HABITS

Recycling containers is just one way consumers worldwide can help reduce hazardous waste—which is part of the solution to the global garbage problem and trade in hazardous materials. Consumers, after all, help determine what kinds of goods are manufactured and sold. If people habitually buy products that are responsible for hazardous waste, they are contributing to a demand for the products and an increase in toxic trash.

In recent years, an increasing number of people have become aware of how some goods and services can create environmental and health hazards and have started to buy from companies that prevent pollution, including contamination from toxic waste. As companies feel the pressure to improve their efforts to protect the environment, they have developed advertising and public relations campaigns to tout their good deeds. But some claims about "being green," or environmentally responsible, are misleading. So how do consumers know which companies to patronize?

There is no simple answer, particularly when it comes to judging large corporations. Petrochemical companies, for example, manufacture a variety of plastic products, and the manufacturing process generates toxic waste. The oil needed to make the plastics may spill from a tanker and create hazards in the sea and on land. But petrochemical companies have supported or established new firms that recycle plastic and make new products, like park benches and roofing shingles.

"Eco-labels" or seals of approval certifying that products have not been manufactured with hazardous materials may help consumers make some choices. Product-labeling programs have been initiated in several European countries, Canada, and the United States. The oldest program is in Germany, where the Institute for Quality Assurance and Labeling issues a Blue Angel seal to products that have been tested and found safe for the environment. Many of the products with the Blue Angel seal are manufactured with recycled materials or may be operated by renewable fuels such as solar energy.

In the United States, a nonprofit Alliance for Social Responsibility in New York City is developing specifications for a Green Seal program. To qualify for the seal, products not only must be "earth-safe" themselves, but they also must be manufactured with clean technology—free of toxic waste. Products also will be tested to determine whether they are durable and whether they can be recycled or repaired.

Another nonprofit organization, the Green Cross Certification Company, has developed an environmental seal of approval that it awards to companies/products that meet such environmental standards as energy efficiency and use of recycled materials. Several major discount store chains, such as Wal-Mart and K-mart, are selling a line of products that carry a "green" sticker or label.

Still there are many debates over the types of products that are truly "green." For example, there is no consensus on whether paper products are always better to use than plastic materials. It is common knowledge that plastic materials clog landfills because they do not biodegrade and may be intact for centuries. Plastic manufacturing also generates hazardous waste. But paper products account for most of the material dumped in landfills, and they are compacted so tightly, without air and light, that they cannot break down either. Paper mills also generate many toxins.

Martin B. Hocking, a chemistry professor at the University of Victoria in British Columbia, compared the manufacture of polystyrene cups with those made with paper. In a report in *Science*, Hocking concluded that plastic cups used fewer raw materials and generated less waste. "Six times as much wood pulp as polystyrene is required to produce a cup," Hocking found, and manufacturing a paper cup consumes much more energy and water. He also noted that resins used to waterproof paper cups make them impossible to recycle.[9]

Because the environmental impacts of products and services are difficult to determine, consumers must be constantly on the alert for as much objective information as possible in order to separate the "good guys" from the "bad guys." Articles on environmental issues, including toxic products and hazardous waste, appear regularly in national magazines, major newspapers, and regional and local publications. Dozens of environmental organizations publish books, newsletters, and packets of educational materials on general or specific environmental topics. Books on how to protect the earth or how to be an activist line many shelves in bookstores and libraries (a few such resources are listed at the end of this book in Further Reading). Many schools and communities also provide educational programs on the environment or conduct projects to clean up hazardous materials or prevent pollution.

"EVERYONE HAS A ROLE"

Yet with all of the educational efforts, legislation, law enforcement, scientific studies, group protests, and public debates on local, national, and international levels, individuals still have to help solve the problem of global garbage and the trade in hazardous wastes and products.

"Everyone has a role" in the process, an EPA pamphlet declares. One way to begin is to reduce the amount or toxicity of the waste materials we generate, following a guide for "Safer Substitutes for Household Hazards," such as the one reprinted on page 120.

Along with reducing waste, we can all reuse products and recycle materials to help eliminate some of the toxic trash and products. "Reduce, reuse, recycle" is a familiar environmental slogan. But the EPA adds another "R-word" to the list: *respond*. Let politicians, merchants, manufacturers, and others know that you prefer nontoxic products and want a community free of hazardous materials.

Individuals can make their voices heard. Like Sitting Bull, who long ago criticized a nation that defaced the land with refuse, some fifteen hundred young people from twenty nations called attention to global degradation of all kinds. The young people, aged seven to twenty-four, attended a Global Youth Forum at the United Nations headquarters in New York and prepared a resolution for delivery to the 1992 Earth Summit. The declaration noted that world leaders have stated repeatedly that youth will have to bear the burdens of environmental problems and find ways to save the earth. But the youth forum called this "a delaying tactic" and demanded that leaders of nations initiate "REAL changes in the world. . . . If you are leaving the future to us, then please leave us the present as well," their resolution pleaded.[10]

SAFER SUBSTITUTES FOR HOUSEHOLD HAZARDS

Hazardous Product	Safer Substitute
All purpose cleaner	In 1 quart warm or hot water, mix 1 teaspoon liquid soap, boric acid (borax), lemon juice, and/or vinegar. Make stronger according to the job to be done.
Glass cleaner	Mix 1 tablespoon vinegar or lemon juice in 1 quart water. Spray on and use newspaper to wipe dry.
Drain cleaner	Pour boiling water down drain once a week. Use a plunger or snake.
Oven cleaner	Clean spills as soon as the oven cools using steel wool and baking soda; for tough stains, add salt (do not use this method in self-cleaning or continuous-clean ovens).
Toilet bowl cleaner	Use a toilet brush and baking soda or vinegar.
Furniture polish	Wipe with mixture of 1 teaspoon lemon oil in 1 pint mineral or vegetable oil.
Rug deodorizer and shampoo	Deodorize dry carpets by sprinkling liberally with baking soda. Wait at least 15 minutes and vacuum. Repeat if necessary. To clean rugs, vacuum first to remove dirt. Mix 1 quart white vinegar and 3 quarts boiling water. Apply to nap of rug with wet rag being careful not to saturate rug backing. Dry thoroughly. Then vacuum.
Plant sprays	Wipe leaves with mild soap and water; rinse.
Roach and ant repellent	Sprinkle powdered boric acid in cabinet edges, around baseboards, and in cracks.
Mothballs	Use cedar chips, lavender flowers, rosemary, mint, or white peppercorns.
Flea and tick removers	Mix brewer's yeast or garlic in your pet's food; sprinkle fennel, rue, rosemary, or eucalyptus seeds or leaves around animal sleeping areas.

Source Notes

CHAPTER ONE

1. Quoted by T. C. McLuhan in *Touch the Earth: A Self-Portrait of Indian Existence* (New York: Simon & Schuster, 1971), 90.
2. Joni Seager, ed., *The State of the Earth Atlas* (New York: Simon & Schuster, 1990), 13.
3. Center for Investigative Reporting and Bill Moyers, *Global Dumping Ground* (Washington, D.C.: Seven Locks Press, 1990), 7.
4. Jim Vallette and Heather Spalding, *The International Trade in Wastes* (Washington, D.C.: Greenpeace U.S.A., 1990), 266–267, 286.
5. Council on Environmental Quality, *U.S. National Report* (draft report prepared for submission to the UN Conference on Environment and Development in 1992, released for public comment May 1991), chap. 5.
6. Joe Thornton, "The Dioxin Deception," *Greenpeace* (May/June 1991), 20.
7. "U.S. Health Aide Says He Erred on Times Beach," *New York Times* (May 26, 1991), A12.
8. Personal correspondence, June 5, 1991.
9. Personal correspondence, June 6, 1991.
10. "Dioxin: Jury Awards $1.5 Million," Econet (electronic news release), July 15, 1991.

11. John Carpi, "Metal Illnesses," *E Magazine* (November–December 1990), 34. Also Kathlyn Gay, *Silent Killers* (New York: Franklin Watts, 1988), chap. 6.
12. Alexandra Greeley, "Getting the Lead Out of Just About Everything," *FDA Consumer* (July–August 1991), 28–29.
13. "Government Steps Up Efforts to Prevent Lead Poisoning," *Chemecology* (February 1991), 10–11.

CHAPTER TWO

1. The Global Tomorrow Coalition, *The Global Ecology Handbook* (Boston: Beacon Press, 1990), 248. Also Council on Environmental Quality, *U.S. National Report*, chap. 5.
2. Council on Environmental Quality, *U.S. National Report*, chap. 3.
3. Gail E. Chehak and Suzan Shown Harjo, "Protection Quandary in Indian Country," *Environmental Action* (January/February 1990), 21–22.
4. Ibid. Also Paul Schneider, "Other People's Trash," *Audubon* (July/August 1991), 109–119; Bradley Angel, "Indians Resist Toxic Invasion," *Greenpeace* (September/October 1990), 24.
5. Daphne Wysham, "Who Owns Alaska?" *Greenpeace* (July/August 1991), 10–17.

CHAPTER THREE

1. "Only the Ruthless and Greedy Need Apply," *World Press Review* (November 1988), 32.
2. Jim Vallette and Heather Spalding, eds., *The International Trade in Wastes* (Washington, D.C.: Greenpeace U.S.A., 1990), Preface.
3. James Painter, "Paraguayans Balk at Lucrative Trash

Deal From New York City," *Christian Science Monitor* (January 9, 1990), 5.

4. Tyler Marshall, "Public Spurs Cleanup: West Europe Has Its Fill of Toxic Waste," *Los Angeles Times* (February 28, 1989), 1. Also Center for Investigative Reporting and Bill Moyers, *Global Dumping Ground* (Washington, D.C.: Seven Locks Press, 1990), 1–2; Vallette and Spalding, *The International Trade in Wastes,* 334–346.
5. Greenpeace Waste Trade Project news release, March 27, 1991.
6. *Global Dumping Ground*, 52.
7. Michael Satchell, "Poisoning the Border," *U.S. News & World Report* (May 6, 1991), 33–41.
8. Quoted by Dianne Dumanoski in "U.S. Firms in Mexico Cited as Big Polluters," *Boston Globe* (May 10, 1991), sec. 3, p. 4. Also Sandy Tolan, "Border Boom," *New York Times Magazine* (July 1, 1990), 18–21, 31, 40.
9. Giff Johnson, "Marshall Islands Hope to Profit on Imported Garbage," *Los Angeles Times* (May 7, 1989), sec. 1, p. 2.
10. Greenpeace International Waste Trade Project, *Pollution for the Marshall Islands Equals Profits for the U.S.* (Washington, D.C.: Greenpeace U.S.A., June 1990).
11. Andreas Bernstorff and Jim Puckett, *Poland: The Waste Invasion: A Greenpeace Dossier* (Washington, D.C.: Greenpeace International Waste Trade Campaign), October 11, 1990.
12. Ibid.

CHAPTER FOUR

1. William A. McClenaghan, *Magruder's American Government*, 67th ed., rev. (Newton, MA: Allyn and Bacon, 1987), 361, 418.
2. United Nations Environment Programme, *Basel Convention on the Control of Transboundary Movements of Haz-*

ardous Wastes and Their Disposal: Final Act (Basel, Switzerland: UNEP, March 22, 1989).
3. Edward Cody, "105 Nations Back Treaty on Toxic-Waste Shipping," *Washington Post* (March 23, 1989), A1.
4. Jim Vallette and Heather Spalding, *The International Trade in Wastes: A Greenpeace Inventory*, 5th ed. (Washington, D.C.: Greenpeace U.S.A., 1990), 15–16.
5. Ibid, 11. Also Center for Investigative Reporting and Bill Moyers, *Global Dumping Ground* (Washington, D.C.: Seven Locks Press, 1990), 14.
6. "Africa Adopts Sweeping Measures to Protect Continent from Toxic Terrorism," *Greenpeace Waste Trade Update* (March 22, 1991), 1.
7. Greenpeace Waste Trade Project, "The Gods Must Be Crazy: Mercury Wastes Dumped by Thor in South Africa," A Greenpeace International Waste Trade Profile, April 10, 1990.
8. Peter H. Sand, "Innovations in International Environmental Governance," *Environment* (November 1990), 20, 40.

CHAPTER FIVE

1. Joseph LaDou, "Deadly Migration," *Technology Review* (July 1991), 48.
2. Jonathan Dahl, "Canada Encourages Mining of Asbestos, Sells to Third World," *Wall Street Journal* (September 12, 1989), A1, A16.
3. Christopher Scanlan, "U.S. Industrial Giants Continue Fueling Lead to Third World," *Oregonian* (June 16, 1991), R13.
4. Curtis C. Travis and Sheri T. Hester, "Global Chemical Pollution," *Environmental Science & Technology* (May 1991), 817.

5. Morton Mintz, "Tobacco Roads: Delivering Death to the Third World," *Progressive* (May 1991), 24.
6. Frank Viviano, "Taiwan Is Fuming over American Cigaret Ads," *San Francisco Chronicle* (September 3, 1989), Sunday Punch sec., p. 7. Also Christopher Scanlan, "U.S. Peddles Toxic Items to Third World," *Oregonian* (May 26, 1991), A1, A5.
7. As quoted by Morton Mintz in "Tobacco Roads: Delivering Death to the Third World," *Progressive* (May 1991), 28.
8. Foundation for Advancements in Science and Education, "Exporting Banned and Hazardous Pesticides," Supplement to *FASE Reports* (Winter/Spring 1991), S1.
9. Joni Seager, ed., *The State of the Earth Atlas* (New York: Simon & Schuster, 1990), 105.
10. Ibid., 32.
11. "Exporting Banned and Hazardous Pesticides," Supplement to *FASE Reports*, S1–S2.
12. Ibid.
13. "Dangerous Residues of Extremely Toxic Pesticide Found in Bananas," Pesticide Action Network news release, June 7, 1991.
14. Quoted in "US EPA to Ban Parathion," news release from Pesticide Action Network, North American Regional Center, July 11, 1991.
15. Board on Agriculture of the National Research Council, *Alternative Agriculture* (Washington, D.C.: National Academy Press, 1989) 175–189. Also Kathlyn Gay, *Cleaning Nature Naturally* (New York: Walker & Company, 1991), chaps. 2, 3.
16. *FASE Reports*, S8.
17. Quoted by Robert L. Jackson in "Senate Panel Hears of Pesticide Harm Abroad," *Los Angeles Times* (June 6, 1991), A4.
18. Ibid.

CHAPTER SIX

1. News Releases from the Northern European Nuclear Information Group via Econet (electronic service), June 8, June 24, 1991.
2. "Controversial Incineration-at-Sea Site in Gulf of Mexico Officially Closed by EPA," *BNA Environment Daily* (electronic version from the Bureau of National Affairs), March 8, 1991.
3. "Gulf of Mexico to Receive Added Protection," *Coastal Connection* (Spring 1991 newsletter by the Center for Marine Conservation), 2.
4. Linda Kanamine, "Sewage Contamination Continues to be Major Problem," *USA Today* (May 24, 1991), A7.
5. Quoted by Andy Dabilis in "Cape Ann Crewmen Net Fish and Foul Toxics Come with Catches," *Boston Globe* (February 10, 1991), 23.
6. Jim Vallette and Heather Spalding, *The International Trade in Wastes: A Greenpeace Inventory* (Washington, D.C.: Greenpeace U.S.A., 1990), 202–204.
7. Ibid, 206–207.
8. Daphne Wysham, "Who Owns Alaska?" *Greenpeace* (July/August 1991), 15.
9. Francisco Conde, "Viral Epidemic Suspected in Dolphin Deaths Off Spain," *Los Angeles Times* (September 16, 1990), A20.
10. Peter Verschoor, United Press International news story (electronic service), March 7, 8, 1990. Also Roland De Ligny, Associated Press news story, March 8, 1990; Agence France-Presse, " 'Marine Chernobyl' Strangling North Sea," *San Francisco Chronicle* (August 2, 1988), A12.
11. Econet (electronic service) news release, Oct. 27, 1990.

CHAPTER SEVEN

1. Bill Turque and John McCormick, "The Military's Toxic Legacy," *Newsweek* (August 6, 1990), 20.

2. Lenny Siegel, Gary Cohen, and Ben Goldman, *The U.S. Military's Toxic Legacy: A Special Report on America's Worst Environmental Enemy* (Boston: National Toxic Campaign Fund, 1991).
3. Douglas Frantz, "Toxic Waste Cleanup to Cost Billions," *Los Angeles Times* (June 17, 1990), A31.
4. John M. Broder, "Pollution 'Hot Spots' Taint Water Source," *Los Angeles Times* (June 18, 1990), A16.
5. "Japanese Group Sues U.S. Navy," news release from Foreign Bases Project, Brooklyn, N.Y., June 25, 1991.
6. Bengt Danielsson, "Poisoned Pacific: The Legacy of French Nuclear Testing," *Bulletin of the Atomic Scientists* (March 1990), 24–25.
7. Andre Carothers, "Moruroa Mon Amour: France Tests the World's Patience," *Greenpeace* (January/February 1989), 8.
8. Tilman Ruff, "Bomb Tests Attack the Food Chain," *Bulletin of the Atomic Scientists* (March 1990), 32.
9. Susan E. Davis, "The Battle over Johnson Atoll," *Washington Post* (April 9, 1991), Health sec., p. 7.

CHAPTER EIGHT

1. Martin W. Holdgate, "Antarctica Ice Under Pressure," *Environment* (October 1990), 8.
2. Michael D. Lemonick with Andrea Dorfman, "Antarctica," *Time* (January 15, 1990), 61.
3. Paul Mylrea, "Waste, Pollution Threaten Antarctica, but Conditions Are Improving," *Los Angeles Times* (May 26, 1991), A5. Also "Support Is Growing for Antarctica World Park," *EDF Letter* (February 1991), 8; "EDF News Briefs," *EDF Letter* (June 1991), 2; William Booth, "Face-Off Forming on Antarctic Ice," *Washington Post* (September 28, 1990), A25.
4. Dana K. Harmon, "Old Messes, New Attitudes," *Greenpeace* (July/August 1991), 25.

5. Holdgate, "Antarctica Ice Under Pressure," 30–33.
6. Robert Hennelly, "The End of Antarctica?" *The Earth Care Annual 1991*, 106 (reprinted from the *Christian Science Monitor*, February 7, 1990).
7. Ibid, 108. Also Karin Davies, "Antarctica," United Press International news story filed October 9, 1990, electronic information service.
8. Boyce Rensberger, "Disaster Narrowly Averted in Antarctic Ship Sinking," *Washington Post* (February 4, 1989), A17.
9. Ibid. Also "Oil Fouls Antarctic Ice," *Washington Post* (February 3, 1989), A20; Michael Parfit, "Human Society Carries Trouble to the Bottom of the World," *Los Angeles Times* (February 12, 1989), A1; Jane E. Brody, "In Antarctica, New Threats to the Fragile Web of Life," *New York Times* (February 14, 1989), B5.
10. "Blind on Antarctica," *New York Times* (June 30, 1991), E14.
11. Larry B. Stammer, "Bush Alters Stand, OKs Antarctica Mining Ban," *Los Angeles Times* (July 4, 1991), A26.

CHAPTER NINE

1. Mark D. Uehling, "Tackling the Menace of Space Junk," *Popular Science* (July 1990), 82.
2. Jonathan Eberhart, "Tallying Orbital Trash," *Science News* (July 14, 1990), 29.
3. Gay E. Canough and Lawrence P. Lehman, "What Goes Around, Comes Around: What to Do About Space Debris?" *Analog* (March 1991), 58.
4. Harry F. Rosenthal, Associated Press, "Report Warns of Space Debris' Risk to Future Flights," *Philadelphia Inquirer*, October 12, 1990, A14.
5. Mark D. Uehling, "Tackling the Menace of Space Junk," *Popular Science* (July 1990), 83.
6. "LDEF's Battered Body," *Sky & Telescope* (July 1990), 14.

7. Uehling, "Tackling the Menace of Space Junk," 83.
8. "Space Junk: Fears and Fallacies," *Sky & Telescope* (June 1991), 581. Also *Chicago Tribune* Wire Services, " 'Junkyard' in Space Threatens Missions," *Chicago Tribune* (October 14, 1990), 20.
9. Steven Aftergood, David W. Hafemeister, Oleg F. Prilutsky, Joel R. Primack, and Stanislav N. Rodionov, "Nuclear Power in Space," *Scientific American* (June 1991), 44.
10. Bhupendra Jasani and Martin Rees, "The Junkyard in Orbit," *Bulletin of the Atomic Scientists* (October 1989), 24.

CHAPTER TEN

1. Ricardo Bayon, "The Blame? Who Cares?" *Network '92*, electronic newsletter of the Centre for Our Common Future, December 1990.
2. Council on Environmental Quality, *U.S. Report* (draft), chap. 4.
3. Barnaby J. Feder, "In the Clutches of the Superfund Mess," *New York Times* (June 16, 1991), secs. 1, 3, 6. Also Keith Schneider, "Toxic Pollution Stalls Transfer of Military Sites," *New York Times* (July 18, 1991), A1.
4. Ken Geiser, "Preventing Pollution," *Toxic Watch* (Summer 1990), 1, 7.
5. Bruce Piaseki and Peter Asmus, *In Search of Environmental Excellence* (New York, London, and Toronto: Simon & Schuster, 1990), 143–145.
6. Scott McMurray, "Chemical Firms Find That It Pays to Reduce Pollution at Source," *Wall Street Journal* (June 11, 1991), A1.
7. Ginny Carroll, "Green for Sale," *National Wildlife* (January/February, 1991), 27.
8. Alair Maclean, "Packaging Abroad," *Environmental Action* (March/April 1991), 29.

9. Martin B. Hocking, "Paper versus Polystyrene: A Complex Choice," *Science* (February 1, 1991), 504–505.
10. Quoted by Phil Dunsky, "U.N. Youth Forum Demonstrates 'Carpe Diem' [seize the present]," Environment News Service (electronic service), June 11, 1991.

Further Reading

BOOKS AND REPORTS

Bernstorff, Andreas, and Jim Puckett. *Poland: The Waste Invasion.* Amsterdam, Netherlands: Greenpeace International, 1990.

Bullard, Robert D. *Dumping in Dixie: Race, Class and Environmental Quality.* Boulder, Colo.: Westview Press, 1990.

Bulloch, David K. *The Wasted Ocean.* New York: Lyons and Burford, 1989.

Center for Investigative Reporting and Bill Moyers. *Global Dumping Ground.* Washington, D.C.: Seven Locks Press, 1990.

Cohen, Gary, and John O'Connor, Eds. *Fighting Toxics: A Manual for Protecting Your Family, Community and Workplace.* Washington, D.C.: Island Press, 1990.

Council on Environmental Quality. *U.S. National Report* (a draft). Washington, D.C.: Council on Environmental Quality, 1991.

Environmental Protection Agency. *Toxics in the Community.* Washington, D.C.: EPA, 1990.

Gay, Kathlyn. *Cleaning Nature Naturally.* New York: Walker & Company, 1991.

———. *Garbage and Recycling.* Hillsdale, N.J.: Enslow Publishers, 1991.

———. *Silent Killers.* New York: Franklin Watts, 1988.
———. *Water Pollution.* New York: Franklin Watts, 1990.
Global Tomorrow Coalition. *The Global Ecology Handbook.* Boston: Beacon Press, 1990.
Gupta, Avijit. *Ecology and Development in the Third World.* London and New York: Routledge, 1988.
Kamel, Rachael. *The Global Factory.* Philadelphia: American Friends Service Committee, 1990.
Kenworth, Lauren, and Eric Shaefer. *A Citizen's Guide to Promoting Toxic Waste Reduction.* New York: INFORM, 1990.
National Toxic Campaign Fund. *The U.S. Military's Toxic Legacy: America's Worst Environmental Enemy* (Executive Summary). Boston: National Toxic Campaign Fund, 1991.
National Toxics Campaign. *Fighting Toxics.* Washington, D.C.: Island Press, 1990.
Office of Technology Assessment. *From Pollution to Prevention; A Progress Report on Waste Reduction.* Washington, D.C.: U.S. Government Printing Office, 1987.
O'Hara, Kathryn J. *A Citizens Guide to Plastics in the Ocean: More Than a Litter Problem.* Washington, D.C.: Center for Marine Conservation, 1988.
Piasecki, Bruce, and Peter Asmus. *In Search of Environmental Excellence.* New York and London: Simon & Schuster, 1990.
Seager, Joni, Editor. *The State of the Earth Atlas.* New York and London: Simon & Schuster, 1990.
United Nations Environment Programme. *Basel Convention on the Control of Transboundary Movement of Hazardous Wastes and Their Disposal: Final Act.* Nairobi, Kenya: UNEP, 1989.
U.S. Environmental Protection Agency. *Report of Audit: EPA's Program to Control Exports of Hazardous Waste.* Washington, D.C.: U.S. EPA, 1988.
U.S. Environmental Protection Agency. *Report of Audit: EPA's Program to Control Exports of Hazardous Waste* (Follow-up). Washington, D.C.: U.S. EPA, 1990.

Vallette, Jim, and Heather Spalding. *The International Trade in Wastes: A Greenpeace Inventory*. Washington, D.C.: Greenpeace U.S.A., 1990.

Weir, David, and Mark Schapiro. *Circle of Poison*. San Francisco: Institute for Food and Development Policy, 1981.

Wild, Russell, ed. *The Earth Care Annual 1992*. Emmaus, Pa: Rodale Press, 1992.

PERIODICALS

Aftergood, Steven, David W. Hafemeister, Oleg F. Prilutsky, Joel R. Primack, and Stanislav N. Rodionov. "Nuclear Power in Space," *Scientific American*, June 1991, pp. 42–47.

Baker, Beth. "Testing the Waters." *Common Cause*, January/February 1991, pp. 22–27.

"Beyond White Environmentalism." *Environmental Action*, January/February 1990 (special section on Minorities & the Environment), pp. 19–30.

"Big Eye on Space Debris." *Sky & Telescope*, October 1990, p. 348.

Booth, William. "Face-Off Forming on Antarctic Ice." *Washington Post*, September 28, 1990, p. A25.

Broder, John M. "Toxic Waste: A Federal Failure." *Los Angeles Times*, a series beginning June 17, 1990.

Brody, Jane E. "In Antarctica, New Threats to the Fragile Web of Life." *New York Times*, pp. B5, B10.

"Canada's Green Plan: Blueprint for a Healthy Environment." *Environment*, May 1991, pp. 14–20, 38–45.

Canough, Gay E., and Lawrence P. Lehman. "What Goes Around, Comes Around: What to Do about Space Debris?" *Analog Science Fiction/Science Fact*, March 1991, pp. 54–67.

Carroll, Ginny. "Green For Sale." *National Wildlife*, January/February 1991, pp. 24–27.

Chepesiuk, Ron. "From Ash to Cash: The International

Trade in Toxic Waste." *E Magazine*, July/August 1991, pp. 31–37, 63.
Choucri, Nazli. "The Global Environment and Multinational Corporations." *Technology Review*, April 1991, pp. 52–59.
Christrup, Judy. "Of Apartheid and Pollution." *Greenpeace*, May/June, 1991, pp. 18–19.
Christrup, Judy, and Robert Schaeffer. "Not in Anyone's Backyard." *Greenpeace*, January/February, 1990, pp. 14–19.
Cowen, Ron. "LDEF Maps Orbiting Junk." *Science News*, June 15, 1991, p. 381.
Dahl, Jonathan. "Canada Encourages Mining of Asbestos, Sells to Third World." *Wall Street Journal*, September 12, 1989, pp. A1, A16.
Danielsson, Bengt. "Poisoned Pacific: The Legacy of French Nuclear Testing." *Bulletin of the Atomic Scientists*, March 1990, pp. 22–31.
Davis, Susan E. "The Battle over Johnson Atoll." *Washington Post*, April 9, 1991, p. Z7.
Dumanoski, Dianne. "U.S. Firms in Mexico Cited as Big Polluters." *Boston Globe*, May 10, 1991, p. 4.
Dye, Lee. "Bits of Orbiting Debris Pose Potential Hazard to Future Missions." *Los Angeles Times*, March 5, 1990, p. B2.
Eberhart, Jonathan. "Tallying Orbital Trash." *Science News*, July 14, 1990, p. 29.
"Eco-tourism Takes on Cruise-Garbage Issue." *Chicago Tribune*, November 25, 1990, Travel Section, p. 4.
Feder, Barnaby J. "In the Clutches of the Superfund Mess." *New York Times*, June 16, 1991, sec. 3, pp. 1, 6.
Frosch, Robert A., and Nicholas E. Gallopoulos. "Strategies for Manufacturing." *Scientific American*, September 1989, pp. 144–152.
Garrett, Laurie. "The Toxic Trashing of Central America." *Newsday*, January 15, 1991, p. 59.

Further Reading

"Global Trade in the 90s." *Harvard International Review*, Summer 1991.

Graham, Frank, Jr. "U.S. and Soviet Environmentalists Join Forces across the Bering Strait." *Audubon*, July/August 1991, pp. 43–61.

Hall, Alan, with Emily T. Smith and John Carey. "The World's Frozen Clean Room." *Business Week*, January 22, 1990, pp. 72–76.

Hamilton, Martha M. "Environmental Entrepreneurs Cleaning Up." *Washington Post*, October 22, 1990, p. F1.

Holdgate, Martin W. "Antarctica: Ice Under Pressure." *Environment*, October 1990, pp. 5–9, 30–33.

Jaffe, Mark. "Ash Is Gone, but Freighter Continues Its Troubled Course." *Philadelphia Inquirer*, October 28, 1989, p. B1.

———. "A Growing Debate over Waste Ash." *Philadelphia Inquirer*, March 6, 1988, p. C1.

———. "Haiti Is the Latest to Reject City Ash." *Philadelphia Inquirer*, February 2, 1988, p. B4.

———. "The West's Latest Export: Unwanted Waste." *Philadelphia Inquirer*, March 6, 1989, p. C1.

Jaffe, Mark, and Paul Scicchitano. "Pier Can't Take Ship's Cargo of Ash." *Philadelphia Inquirer*, March 6, 1988, p. A1.

Jasani, Bhupendra, and Martin Rees. "The Junkyard in Orbit." *Bulletin of the Atomic Scientists*, October 1989, pp. 24–25, 39.

Johnson, Giff. "Marshall Islands Hope to Profit on Imported Garbage." *Los Angeles Times*, May 7, 1989, p. A2.

Juffer, June. "Dump at the Border." *Progressive*, October 1988, pp. 24–29.

LaDou, Joseph. "Deadly Migration: Hazardous Industries' Flight to the Third World." *Technology Review*, July 1991, pp. 47–53.

Laver, Ross. "Who Pays the Bill?" *Maclean's*, September 17, 1990, pp. 76–78.

Lemonick, Michael D. "Antarctica." *Time*, January 15, 1990, pp. 56–62.

Levenson, Howard. "Wasting Away: Policies to Reduce Trash Toxicity and Quantity." *Environment*, March 1990, pp. 10–15, 30–36.

Linnerooth, Joanne, and Allen V. Kneese. "Hazardous Waste Management: A West German Approach." *Resources*, Summer 1989, pp. 7–10.

MacNeill, Jim. "Strategies for Sustainable Economic Development." *Scientific American*, September 1989, pp. 155–175.

Marshall, Tyler. "Europe Grappling with Hazardous Waste Crisis." *San Francisco Chronicle*, March 8, 1989, p. 9.

———. "West Europe Has Its Fill of Toxic Waste." *Los Angeles Times*, February 28, 1989, p. A1.

McMurray, Scott. "Chemical Firms Find That It Pays to Reduce Pollution at Source." *Wall Street Journal*, June 11, 1991, pp. A1, A6.

Mintz, Morton. "Tobacco Roads: Delivering Death to the Third World." *Progressive*, May 1991, pp. 24–29.

Montague, Peter. "Earthly Necessities: A New Environmentalism for the 1990s." *Workbook*, Summer 1991, pp. 50–62.

Morain, Dan. "Complex, Costly Cleanups May Snarl Base Closings." *Los Angeles Times*, June 19, 1990, p. A1.

"Ocean Disposal Reconsidered" (collection of articles). *Oceanus*, Summer 1990, entire issue.

Painter, James. "Paraguayans Balk at Lucrative Trash Deal from New York City." *Christian Science Monitor*, January 9, 1990, p. 5.

Parfit, Michael. "Human Society Carries Trouble to the Bottom of the World." *Los Angeles Times*, February 12, 1989, pt. 5, p. 1.

Park, Robert. "Do We Want Chernobyls in the Sky?" *Washington Post*, February 26, 1989, p. C3.

Pesticide Action Network North American Alliance. "New Coalition Promotes Social Justice in Maquiladoras." Electronic News Bulletin, June 4, 1991.
"Radioactive Space Debris Study Cites Hazards to Satellites, Earth." *Aviation Week & Space Technology*, September 22, 1986, pp. 19–20.
Raskin, Frances. "Ocean Watch." *Friends of the Earth*, October 1990, pp. 12–13.
"Recycling: How to Throw Things Away." *Economist*, April 13, 1991, pp. 17–22.
Rensberger, Boyce. "Disaster Narrowly Averted in Antarctic Ship Sinking." *Washington Post*, February 4, 1989, p. A17.
Robie, David. "Rising Storm in the Pacific." *Greenpeace*, January/February 1989, pp. 6–10.
Ruff, Tilman. "Bomb Tests Attack the Food Chain." *Bulletin of the Atomic Scientists*, March 1990, pp. 32–34.
Sand, Peter H. "Innovations in International Environmental Governance." *Environment*, November 1990, pp. 16–20, 40–43.
Satchell, Michael. "Poisoning the Border." *U.S. News & World Report*, May 6, 1991, pp. 33–41.
Sawyer, Kathy. "Orbiting Litter Poses Risk to Space Ventures." *Washington Post*, June 19, 1989, p. A3.
Scanlan, Christopher. "U.S. Industrial Giants Continue Fueling Lead to Third World." *Sunday Oregonian*, June 16, 1991, p. R13.
———. "U.S. Peddles Toxic Items to Third World." *Sunday Oregonian*, May 26, 1991, pp. A1, A5.
Schneider, Keith. "Toxic Pollution Stalls Transfer of Military Sites." *New York Times*, July 18, 1991, p. A1.
Schneider, Paul. "Other People's Trash." *Audubon*, July/August 1991, pp. 108–119.
Schwartz, John, with Carla Koehl and Karen Breslau. "Cleaning Up by Cleaning Up." *Newsweek*, June 11, 1990, pp. 40–41.
Small, Jill. "Greenpeace Reveals New Jersey Mercury

Waste Shipped to Spain." Greenpeace News Release, March 27, 1991.
Stammer, Larry B. "Bush Alters Stand, OKs Antarctica Mining Ban." *Los Angeles Times*, July 4, 1991, p. A26.
Tolan, Sandy. "Border Boom." *New York Times Magazine*, July 1, 1990, pp. 17–21, 31, 40.
Travis, Curtis C., and Sheri T. Hester. "Global Chemical Pollution." *Environmental Science & Technology*, May 1991, pp. 814–819.
Turque, Bill, and John McCormick. "The Military's Toxic Legacy." *Newsweek*, August 6, 1990, pp. 20–23.
Uehling, Mark D. "Tackling the Menace of Space Junk." *Popular Science*, July 1990, pp. 82–85, 92.
Wallace, Charles P. "Toxic Waste Dumping Threatens Third World." *San Francisco Chronicle*, April 4, 1991, p. A15.
Weingarten, Paul. "Long Trip Turns Satellite into a Scientist's Dream." *Chicago Tribune*, January 14, 1990, p. 1.
"Where There's Muck There's High Technology." *Economist*, April 8, 1989, pp. 24–26.
Williams, Jeffery D. "Trashing Developing Nations: The Global Hazardous Waste Trade." *Buffalo Law Review*, Winter 1991, pp. 275–307.
Wysham, Daphne. "Who Owns Alaska?" *Greenpeace*, July/August 1991, pp. 10–15.
Yakowitz, Harvey. "Global Hazardous Transfers." *Environmental Science Technology*, May 1989, pp. 510–511.

Index

Index

Index

Index